Wild Friends

A True Story
of Life with Animal Orphans

by Rae Perry

Gannett Books
PORTLAND, MAINE

DEDICATED TO:

My husband Tom;
   Who has had animals in his hair, his bed and at times in his bath.

My sons Chuck & Bruce;
   Their childhood was an unusual learning experience and they have pretty much forgiven me for it.

My daughter-in-law Debbie;
   Her interest and love of the orphans has given me a double blessing.

My grandson Eric;
   May your eyes also see the wonders of nature and your heart rejoice in the presence of her children.

SPECIAL THANKS

To Maine's Wardens for sharing your knowledge of the wildlife with me.

To my friend Lola; my mentor to the written word.

And, those who shared the photos and snapshots for this family album of my wild orphan friends.

Photo Credits

My thanks to these friends for their
snapshots and photos that helped make
this a real family photo album.

Orman and Cosbrove, Houston, Texas

Linda Ely, Camden, Maine

K.G. Rolerson, Warren, Maine

Carolyn Warren, Morrill, Maine

Crystal Stone, Appleton, Maine

Christine Ludwig, Hope, Maine

Laurine Lee Clayton, Camden, Maine

Table of Contents

Chapter 1
My Own Bambi

Animals, domestic and wild, have been a part of my life as long as I can remember.

I grew up on a wonderful old farm in Warren, Maine. My father raised replacement heifers for dairy farms and my mother raised Cocker Spaniels.

As an infant I developed an allergy to cow's milk, so my father traded a heifer for several milk goats.

When I was old enough to be placed outdoors in my playpen, I became the object of interest for the nanny goats and several of the dogs.

My first baby steps were guided by the bodies of the goats and several of the dogs. When I tumbled, their legs and necks made excellent hand-holds for me to pull myself back up to a standing position. I was an only child, but I never again walked alone.

In the spring of my seventh year, my dad went to help a neighbor find a cow that had apparently calved, as she didn't return with the rest of the herd at milking time. Our neighbor, Chet, had taken his Scottie dog along to help scent out the cow if she was hiding in a thicket.

As my dad and Chet walked the pasture, they passed one of the many small areas consisting of scrub pine and running juniper. Suddenly the Scottie dashed into the thicket. Before the men could react, a deer came stumbling out of the underbrush with the dog ripping and tearing at its throat. As Chet pursued the struggling deer and his dog, my dad crawled into the thicket, following the trail the deer had left. Daddy realized that a small dog like the Scottie couldn't have attacked the deer at the throat unless it was laying down. Why the deer didn't immedi-

Here I am, learning about life on a farm in Maine.

When I fell down, the goats helped me get back up.

ately jump up and run soon became apparent. There were two fawns, one still half covered with afterbirth.

While my father stood guard over the two helpless fawns, Chet and his Scottie dog hurried to the nearest phone to call the local game warden. Wardens will tell you that this is not an isolated incident. Domesticated dogs, our housepets, kill more deer and fawns than any "natural" predator.

When Daddy came home with Warden White, I went running out to see what they had in their arms. Being only seven, my sole acquaintance with fawns was the storybook tale of Bambi. I was completely overwhelmed by the sight of two fawns. I immediately named them both Bambi.

Our dairy cow and goat farm was in a very rural setting. Our only access was a dirt road with little traffic. My parents owned over 100 acres of pasture and woodland, so it was recognized as an acceptable environment in which to raise the fawns, a doe and a buck.

The first few days were filled with baby bottles and feedings every four hours. At first, the fawns were only allowed two ounces of milk each feeding.

Our newborn fawns weighed four and one-half pounds for the doe and five pounds for the buck. In the wild, does nurse their fawns no more than every four or five hours and then leave them hidden while they browse.

Fawns are practically odorless for their first few weeks of life, which helps to protect them from sharp-nosed predators. If the fawn should wander from where the doe left it, she can track the fawn from a waxy secretion the fawn has left on the earth. This waxy substance comes from the interdigital gland located in the center of the hoof between the toes. If a human is raising a very small fawn, constant vigilance must be maintained, for if the fawn should become frightened it will immediately hide by lying down and we humans do not have the doe's ability to locate its hiding place by smelling our way to it.

Soon our fawns were exploring our barn, nibbling on wisps of hay as they ambled about. The fawns established genial "nose-to-nose" acquaintance with the calves, but they looked on yearningly as the calves nursed. A step too near and the cow would bellow, sending the fawns racing back to the security of their pen.

The fawns soon discovered that "milking time" occurred twice a day. At the first sound of milk pinging into the milk pail, kittens would magically appear, as if out of the very walls. The kittens would sit in a line waiting patiently for my father to send a squirt of milk their way, then happily lick the milk from their whiskers, noses and chests.

After milking, the fawns received a foaming pan of milk laced with grain. At first they would "butt" the pan as they drank, making the milk spill out, which immediately made for them fast new friends, the kittens.

Earliest "wild friend," and me.

By June the fawns were out exploring the green pastures and racing through the tall grass of the hay fields.

The doe became increasingly shy and timid, slipping off into the woods for most of the day, only returning at milking time for her supper and her secure pen for the night. This left me to be the buck's companion.

Timid and shy, but friendly.

The buck was Mary's little lamb! Wherever I went, he was sure to follow. He would nibble affectionately at my clothes and if there was a handkerchief to work free, he would tug it loose and trot off with me trying in vain to catch him. He made the rules and the game ended only when he tired of it.

When visitors drove into our yard, he was the first one to greet them with lapping tongue. Men who kept their cigarettes in their shirt pockets would, more often than not, find them missing after Bambi's burst of introductory affection. When next they saw the fawn he would be racing across the lawn with the package of cigarettes in his mouth. Trying to keep Bambi from overdosing on tobacco wasn't easy, as he was so adept at helping himself. He was also very partial to blueberries, raspberries, apples and rock salt.

Bambi had a natural talent for keeping everyone on their toes. One evening, just as we were finishing supper, my father mentioned to my mother that he had left a grain bag full of apples in the shed for her. These were for making apple sauce as well as fresh apples for us. My mother immediately made a beeline for the shed, muttering about dumb men and marauding deer. My father was right behind her, insisting that the apples were safe, and they were Bambi-proof since he had tied the grain bag shut. We found the wooden floor of the shed had been transformed into a beautiful red carpet of apples. In the middle of it all stood Bambi. He had obviously taste-tested several dozen red apples before finally selecting to eat the biggest and reddest of them all. "A very discerning deer, that one," my father said.

By late fall both deer had shed their spotted fawn coats for their winter coats of cinnamon brown. The buck had also acquired "buttons". If a buck has good forage, high in protein, he may even acquire "spike" antlers in his first year.

When a buck is born, he has two swirls of hair on his forehead, showing where the antlers will form as he gets older. At two to three months of age, bony knobs, called the pedicels, start to form on the frontal skull plate. At five to six months of age, the pedicels are about three-quarters of an inch to one inch long and have raised the skin up so that they are very noticeable. At this stage he is known as a "button" buck because of the knobs.

When deer hunting season arrived in November, all our neighbors posted their land in an effort to protect our deer. Hunters who came in from outside the area were informed of the tame deer, and being true sportsmen they all chose to hunt elsewhere.

Bambi found the snow a great adventure. He spent his first snowstorm trying to shake the snowflakes from his head. When he at last tired of this useless pastime, he would grab one of my mittens and run away with it. By that time I had given up trying to catch him. Once he realized I would no longer run after him, he would tease me by running past, just within my reach. I would make a fast grab for my mitten and only get a handful of snow for my efforts.

We spent many a winter day playing in the warm and cozy confines of the barn. One of our games was "hide-n-seek". No matter where I hid—under the hay, in a cluttered corner, or in the grain box—Bambi would find me. Bambi would also hide from me and it wasn't so easy for a human to find him. He would find a dark corner, lie down and curl up, remaining perfectly still. Many times the only way I could find him was to reach into that dark corner and feel for him with my hands.

With the advent of late spring, I was looking forward to the end of school so I could roam the woods and fields with Bambi. The doe had become very shy and timid. She rarely came up to the barn, but chose instead her natural habitat, the woods and fields surrounding our farm.

When not with me, Bambi the buck roamed considerable distances. We began receiving letters and phone calls from people as far away as fifteen miles. Bambi would walk up to any human and proceed to nuzzle them. If he sauntered into someone's dooryard and no one was about, he would frequently knock by hitting his front hoof against the door. If someone were home, Bambi generally received tidbits, and a pat or two for his ingenuity. Bambi had learned this trick the previous fall.

Bayside in barn.

The resumption of school had interrupted our days together, and when he missed me, Bambi attempted to get into our house by striking at the door. Thinking it was a neighbor knocking, my mother would answer the door, only to find the fawn bounding past her, bleating for me as he ran from room to room. My mother would give him an apple or other treat as she pushed him back outside.

Bambi was frequently included on the front pages of the local newspapers, and he did his best to remain newsworthy. One day, he wandered into Thomaston, a center of shopping for the smaller towns. Bambi ambled down the sidewalk, stopping often to be patted. Bambi was walking through the open door of a grocery store when Jim Moore, the local photographer, caught up with him. Mr. Moore got some nice photos of Bambi investigating the store's produce section. After receiving a red apple from the owner, Bambi continued on his way.

Happy times, special times, seem to fly by in the wink of an eye. As fall crept in, summer was saying good-bye, so I would have to say good-bye to Bambi.

My mom and dad had a parent-to-child talk with me late one evening to tell me that Bambi had survived one hunting season. But now, with his extensive roaming, the risk was too great. Bambi still didn't

Bayside resting comfortably.

What's that I hear?

Hiding in the grass.

10

Bayside waiting for supper.

have any fear of man; to him humans meant food and friendship. What an easy kill for a hunter who didn't know he was tame, or worse still, didn't care. Because of the acreage Bambi was now traveling, there wasn't any way our neighbors could protect him as they had the year before. Mom and Dad told me about an island reserved for all wild-born animals who are pets and can no longer reside at their foster homes. My Bambi would be taken there by the Warden Service the last week of October.

The Warden Service called my home on a Friday evening to make the arrangements to pick up the deer the following morning. Being a child of eight, I didn't want to give up my Bambi. At daylight the next morning, Bambi and I were hiding in the woods that surround our farm. How I could protect my Bambi, I didn't know, but I felt that given time I could figure it out. Perhaps someone in the adult world would have a solution once they realized how important Bambi was to me. By mid-morning Bambi and I were resting in our favorite grove of pine trees and eating the sandwiches I had made: cucumber for him, peanut butter for me. Suddenly a man in the uniform of the Maine's Warden Service stepped into our private world. It was the same man who had made my days with Bambi possible, Warden White.

As Warden White sat down upon a tree stump, Bambi went bounding over to greet his friend with nudges and lapping kisses. A friend indeed. The man who had regaled me with his stories of the wildlife was here to take my Bambi away. I'm quite sure Warden White realized he had become the bad guy in this little girl's special world.

He gave me a fleeting smile as he took out his pipe and tobacco. As he tamped his pipe and lit it, he told me of an albino porcupine he had found in South Warren and would I like to go with him and see it for myself tomorrow? I said, "Yes, if Bambi could go with us."

"Now Rae," he said, "You know Bambi must go to the island not just for his own protection, but for the safety of humans as well."

Bucky at five months still loves ear lobes.

Bucky, 2 weeks old, practicing camouflage.

"The safety of humans?" I asked. "But Bambi isn't afraid of humans."

"That's part of the problem, Rae" Warden White said. "Let me ask you some questions and see if you know the answers to them."

"Remember the baby porcupine and the baby squirrel you raised?"

"Yes."

"What happened to them? Why don't you still have them?"

"They grew big." I said, "Daddy and I found them homes with adopted brothers and sisters. But they haven't gone away. I can show you where they live."

"Rae, Bambi is big now and he needs to be with others of his own kind."

"But, Warden White, Bambi can have others of his own kind when he's ready, right here. There are lots of deer around here."

"Rae, that's one of the problems with tame deer. Unlike most of the other wildlife, tame deer bodies are grown up and go wild before their minds are ready to tell them to go wild. Bambi's body is all grown up now, and Bambi is a buck. Rae, can you tell me the difference between a bull and a cow?"

"Yes; a cow is a female and a bull is a male."

"And?" he asked.

"A cow is a heifer until she has a baby. A bull is always a bull and he helps make the babies when he's old enough."

"Can you make a pet of a bull, like you can a cow?" he asked.

"Sometimes, but most of the time you can't."

"Why?" he asked.

"I don't know why. All I know is that you should never trust a bull. They will try to hook you with their horns, throw you on the ground and step on you. Neighbor Ruth's bull trapped the hired man in a corner of the barn, and his horns were so long that they made holes in the wall because he pushed so hard. I can show you the holes. Daddy said the man wasn't killed because he was lucky to fit between the horns."

"He was lucky, Rae," said Warden White, "and that brings us back to the safety of humans regarding Bambi. Bambi is a male, a buck deer, and buck deer use their horns and feet like bulls, especially their feet. Buck deer strike with their front feet, and one strike can easily rip your clothes, as if being cut with scissors, and break some of your ribs at the same time. That can be just the first strike. The strike is fast and swift; you won't realize it's happening until it's over, and that could be too late. Bambi would never harm you Rae, but he might attack grownups, if he felt frightened, or even in play. Bambi plays pretty rough with your daddy, sometimes, doesn't he?"

"Yes," I said.

Warden White continued. "If Bambi should hurt someone, we would have to shoot him. Bambi hasn't any fear of humans and because of that, he can become dangerous to us grownups. The only way you can protect Bambi and the humans he might meet is to keep him shut up in your barn for the rest of his life, or let me take him to the island where he can roam free with the others of his own kind. And in a little while, he'll become what he was meant to be, a wild deer."

The three of us walked slowly home through the colored leaves in the afternoon sun. Bambi rode away with Warden White in the van, and I cried for a long time, lying in the empty deer pen.

In a while, Daddy came and rocked me in his arms. For days we talked about the special times that Bambi had given us. By spring, the hurt of losing my shadow had lessened enough for me to become interested in wildlife again.

Ever since that magical year, orphaned animals, wild and domestic, always found their way to me.

As a young adult I had the challenging opportunity to babysit two eight-week-old black bear cubs for several weeks.

My mother was genuinely surprised by the arrival of the bear cubs, but she had great fun teasing Tom, my future husband. She regaled him with unending stories of what he might find on his side of the bed someday.

Much to my family's surprise, I limited myself to raising our two boys Chuck and Bruce, and domestic animals for about 8 years.

In the early spring of 1969, Tom and I inherited the Perry Homestead. We became the eighth consecutive generation of Perrys to occupy this old farm called Willow-Brook, a farm of 85 acres with fields, woods, pasture land and, most important to my avocation-to-be, a fine brook.

Our sons were thrilled with the old barn, the hay fields, woods and the babbling brook. They wanted calves and piglets to raise, and they couldn't wait to harvest our own hay. Chuck and Bruce were not strangers to haying-time. From the time they turned three they were allowed to help Grandpa Perry hay. Grandpa used a team of horses and brought the hay in loose, and the boys' job was to tramp down the hay as it was pitched up onto the hayrick by the adults.

When I was into my third day of unpacking our possessions, my phone began ringing. It was my father. He was trying to make himself heard over the loud screams of a baby animal that was obviously in the immediate area of his phone.

"Rae," my father shouted, "I need to bring a baby raccoon up to you. I'll be there in 45 minutes. I called first because I wanted to see if you have baby bottles and everything you need for its formula. I can pick that stuff up on the way if you need anything. I'll explain about this raccoon when I get there."

"O.K. Daddy. I'll be waiting for you, and no, I don't need you to pick up anything."

"Good-bye," he hollered, slamming down the phone.

By the time I had located the baby bottles and made the formula, my father drove into our dooryard.

My father came in with a box containing not one critter but two. Just as he was leaving his house, a neighbor drove in with a baby woodchuck, saying his son had shot the mother two days ago, and this baby had managed to crawl his way up out of the den. Also in the box was the baby raccoon, its eyes still sealed shut. I heated the formula for the babies as my father told me the tale of the raccoon.

While having his garage roof repaired the day before, workmen had uncovered a nest of baby raccoons. Daddy called the game warden, who removed the kits, placed them in a box and put them on the ground behind my father's garage. He thought the mother raccoon would locate them when she returned and would carry them off to a new home.

That next morning, my father looked into the box and found all the babies were gone, except one. He reached gently into the box and softly touched the little body. It was so cold to his touch that he thought it was dead until he looked for the rise and fall of its breathing. He immediately brought the raccoon into his kitchen and proceeded to warm it by the brisk rubbing of his hands upon the baby's body. After some long, tense moments, the baby raccoon began to squirm and then slowly but surely began sucking a few drops of milk from the eye dropper Daddy placed upon her tongue. It was then that he brought the waif to our doorstep.

Feeding time.

As I bottle-fed the little raccoon and my father fed the little wood-chuck, he told me that, unlike in the "old days," one was now required to have a license to raise and rehabilitate orphaned wildlife. He had already talked with our local game warden and explained the situation to him. My father had answered his questions about my background, gave him references, and explained where I was now living.

Later that day, I received a phone call from the warden's office giving me temporary permission to raise the orphans, until they could investigate my background and references.

Two weeks later, I received my permit. I was now officially one of the approximately 45 people in Maine who are legally allowed to volunteer their time and resources to rescue, raise and rehabilitate wildlife.

From that auspicious day, orphaned and injured wildlife have been brought to our doorstep not only by the Warden Service and local Humane Society shelters, but by dozens of caring individuals.

I am required to file a detailed report each year listing how many orphans I have taken in, the date that they arrived, their approximate ages and when they were released. The total number of orphans to expect each season is totally unpredictable. Our busiest year to date brought nine raccoons, nine grey squirrels, a duck, three red foxes, two porcupines, a woodchuck, skunk, robin, two cedar-waxwings, a nighthawk, a barn swallow and a sea gull.

The following stories are about some of the more outstanding individuals that have crossed our doorsill over the years.

Bugsy and his sore nose.

Chapter 2
The Orphan Elf

Elf was the youngest raccoon of the dozens we raised. She did have fur, for raccoons are born fully furred. However, there wasn't a mask on her face, or rings on her tail. If she'd had a long, hairless tail and longer snout, she might have passed for a baby opossum.

She consumed a quarter-ounce of formula every three hours around the clock for the first week, until she was strong enough to graduate to a four-hour schedule.

At about the eighth day, traces of her mask began coloring in and at 17 days, faint ring markings began appearing on her tail.

By the second week, she started anticipating the alarm clock by ten minutes. I could easily sleep through the sound of the alarm, but not her screams! From then on it was self-demand feeding. Very shortly she was sleeping through the night about half the time. I hadn't been subjected to such a tough regime since my boys were born.

Elf would be human imprinted. This means that because we took over the role of her parents at a young age, she believed we were her parents and she tried, as human babies do, to emulate our behavior.

After four weeks in our household Elf's eyes opened, so by our calculation she was 48 hours old when she came to us.

Between four and six weeks of age, she put all her energy into trying to gain control of her legs and paws. She succeeded mighty well!

The raccoon has five toes on each foot. The front toes are about as long as each corresponding pad. These toes are almost as dexterous as human fingers. Unlike most other animals, the sense of touch is one

18

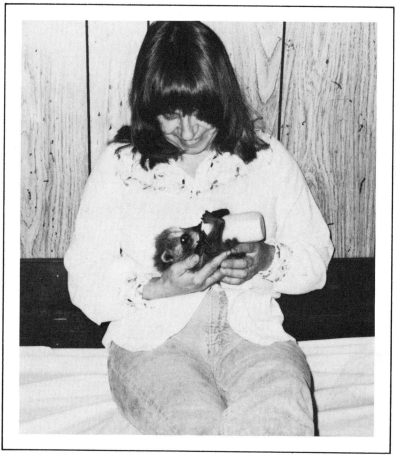

Just a handful of happiness.

of the raccoon's most highly developed senses. Elf was opening cup-board doors, prying into containers, rummaging through every nook and cranny. A mini-tornado of the four-legged variety! By the eighth week, complete havoc was replaced by livable disorder, so long as I didn't rearrange any objects in the house. She usually left most things alone, with the exception of one small item, the sugar bowl. When our backs were turned, Elf would immediately climb onto the counter and make her way to the sugar bowl. She licked her "fingers," dipped them in, and greedily sucked off the sweet stuff. We shortly invested in a can-ning jar-type sugar bowl with a snap-down lit.

At six weeks of age, Elf insisted on sleeping with our teen-age son, Bruce. She had decided that he was her litter-mate or sibling. Every-where Bruce went, Elf demanded to go. Everything he did, she tried to do.

Like any teen-age boy, Bruce tore engines apart; so did Elf. Piston holes were seemingly made specifically for her inquisitive fingers. Grease just magnified the fun. When the two of them came in at night, they each left footprints and pawprints on the porch floor. They were both banished to the tub immediately, Bruce walking barefooted with Elf on his shoulder.

Raccoons love the water and Elf was no exception, but as with all youngsters, soap takes all the fun out of it!

In the wild, water can be more than a playground to a raccoon. Should a dog pursue a full grown raccoon into the water, the dog is in all probability going to perish. If the raccoon succeeds in climbing onto the top of the dog's head, he will grasp the dog's head with its paws. The weight of the raccoon will push the dog's head beneath the water until it drowns, unless he can get to shallow water first.

Elf, like all raccoons, had an excellent sense of smell. Games were invented which gave us all special moments to remember and which developed in Elf some of the talents she would need to assure her future in the wild.

Two of the games were "hide-and-seek" in the tall grass and "follow-me-if-you-can" through the woods.

In the former, one of us would run as fast as we could in a zig-zag manner through the grass, then flop down on the ground and lie per-

I just love blueberries.

fectly still. Elf, being short and not among the most swift of animals, would soon lose sight of us. She then had to put her nose to the ground and "scent-trail" to where we lay in hiding. This is the same manner in which a bloodhound works. Upon reaching us, she would give a leap and hurtle her body onto ours, emitting the most enchanting chirrs and gurgles as she snuggled onto us. Within a few moments she would be up and humping off, leaving us the pursuers!

I thought this would be easy.

All the comforts of home.

Hammocks are tricky.

Corky trying to play "Daddy."

Careful, it's a big world out there.

Irish the setter and Elf.

"Follow-me-if-you-can" evolved during a walk through the woods by Bruce, Elf and me. Elf was bringing up the rear when Bruce decided to step off the path directly behind a large oak tree; then, when Elf and I passed, he jumped out directly behind Elf giving the snorting sound which she used when she tackles a human unexpectedly. Then Elf leaped up and around, landing with her four paws foursquare braced, hackles raised and growling. Almost immediately, she realized it was Bruce and began chirring as she clasped him around his ankles.

In a few moments we resumed our walk, this time with me in the lead, followed by Bruce and Elf bringing up the rear once again. I angled our route so as to pass another good-sized tree and it was I who this time quickly stepped behind the tree and waited. I repeated Bruce's actions, and Elf repeated hers, though not with quite the degree of surprise she showed the first time.

As we resumed our walk, Bruce was in the lead, followed by me and then Elf. Very shortly, Elf started hustling along so as to pass me. I told Bruce I was letting her by and to slow the pace because I thought she wanted the lead. She did.

Let's be friends!

Elf loved Irish, the setter.

Bruce and I ambled along as Elf pushed her rolling sailor's gait to its utmost. Suddenly, she veered off behind a respectable tree. Bruce and I continued on as if we had not noticed her disappearance. As Bruce passed the tree, Elf came galloping out and wrapped all four of her legs around his ankle in one smooth move. A perfect tackle!

Her chirring was at a fever pitch and her black, mischievous eyes were never so bright or full of laughter!

Besides playing in the woods, Elf loved playing in the water, where she soon learned a new hunting skill.

If you ever have lain on the edge of a brook trying to catch frogs, you know the frog will just swim out of reach and then bury himself in the mud on the bottom. The frog's reaction from what I have seen, is completely different when a raccoon is doing the prodding and chasing.

Elf's little paws would knead about the muddy bottom, while her black, shoe-button eyes twinkled with seemingly far-away thoughts of mischief yet to be accomplished. This seems to be standard operating procedure; the action of the face is completely divorced from the action of the paws.

As the movement of her paws came in contact with a frog, a surprising reaction occurred. Instead of the frog swimming across the bottom to escape, it would propel itself straight upward, breaking the surface of the water. In one fluid motion, Elf would sit up on her haunches and catch the frog between her front paws as it left the water. She would then stuff him head first into her mouth.

I personally preferred less gruesome sport, such as trying to halt the flow of a mini-waterfall with nothing but paws and human hands, or trying to catch water beetles.

After a long day of outdoor fun, Elf's favorite form of recreation was to explore visitors' pockets. Many times we watched Elf sit on someone's lap to explore a shirt pocket. She would sit on her haunches, purring and chirring. While one paw caressed the shirt front, the other was deep within the shirt pocket, busily sorting out its contents. Elf removed from one man's shirt pocket a matchbook, examined it minutely with both paws, and then casually dropped it. Reaching again into the pocket, fingers busily searching and feeling, she brought out a penny, examined it, dropped it and returned to the pocket. After removing several more objects, she curled up on his lap and went to sleep. On another occasion, the items she removed, by feel alone, were one matchbook, one penny, one dime, one dollar bill, one nail and one screw. Again the shirt pocket was not empty but Elf was no longer interested. When we checked what she had left this time, we found only duplicates of the objects she had removed. She was not interested in duplicates! Elf demonstrated this ability to sort by feeling numerous times and never ceased to amaze us with this display!

Raccoons have a different wake-and-sleep schedule at maturity than humans. They are most active from 6 p.m. to 10 or 11 p.m. Then again from 2 a.m. to 6 a.m. Elf was now following a wild raccoon's natural habit, sleeping more in the daytime. Quite often, she slept on her back, legs askew and snoring!

With September came new routines. Elf was left outdoors after the barn chores were done. She objected strenuously to this idea. For the first week she would come to the door several times during the night, crying and screaming, and sometimes giving her panic call which is something like a two-note, owlish hoot. I also slept fitfully. My ''baby,'' not knowing that she was supposed to be a nature's child, was out alone in the big, bad world. I did realize it was necessary and for the best, but it's almost impossible to be strictly objective at such times. It was necessary for her to begin to come to terms with her species' needs and with our needs as well.

All wildlife, no matter how young they are when introduced to human association, must eventually succumb to their own traits. A seemingly loving, docile animal will in all likelihood eventually attack its owner to some degree.

My husband Tom is a natural early riser. He would let Elf in at 4:30 a.m. After eating and playing with him, she would thunder up the stairs and hurtle into bed with me. After examining my face, eyes and ears with her fingers, all to the tune of delighted chirrings, she would wiggle under the blankets, snuggle and purr and eventually fall asleep.

Around 6 a.m., Elf and I would crawl out of bed to start another day.

By 6:30 a.m. I would holler to the boys to get up and get ready for school. Elf would dash up the stairs to help Chuck and Bruce with the task. Helping consisted of wriggling and humping about under the blankets so that in no time they were on the floor. If they tried to roll the blankets tightly about themselves, she simply grabbed the covers and un-rolled them.

I began to depend on Elf for ''wake-up'' call. If I was busy in the kitchen, I often told Elf ''go wake Chuck and Bruce'' and off she would cheerfully go. Is there a human anywhere who cannot be awakened when being prodded by a very determined raccoon? If you refuse to let missing blankets, sheets and pillow deter you from sleep, then a raccoon's fingers in your ear, pinching your nose and snuffling in your ear certainly will. Extreme measures call for twisting toes and tickling feet.

I came to rely on Elf. I enjoyed not having to be the ''bossy'' mom, and I especially enjoyed hearing the uproar that was caused by one very small raccoon determined to awaken her playmates.

About once a month, I would suddenly realize that things were not on schedule. A glance at the clock would reveal it was too late for the boys to get up, get dressed and walk to the school bus turnaround. In retrospect, we found that Elf had sensed a fine sunny day dawning and had snuggled in with Bruce. When they all awoke, they had a fine day in which to enjoy favorite pastimes together. I only wish Elf could have understood the difficulties I had in explaining the reason for the boys' absence to an incredulous school principal.

I'm getting tired, Rae.

Elf shares a secret with Irish.

On one of Elf's "let-me-have-my-brothers-to-myself" days, I ordered a "clean-your-room" day, right down to the bare walls. When the boys moved one of the bureaus, they found a bonanza! Elf had a "stash" of her favorite trinkets. Two initialed brass belt buckles belonging to Chuck and Bruce, one necklace (mine), one cuff-link (Tom's), one dollar and sixty cents in change and several of her own small toys. Is the old wives' tale that raccoons will hide shiny objects true? In Elf's case, a most definite "yes."

As late fall settled in, Elf wasn't at the door every morning. Sometimes it was 10 a.m. or later when she appeared, or not at all. As she hadn't developed any shyness toward humans, we often feared for her life. In the fall, there is a legal hunting season for raccoons in Maine.

We know where it's safe.

I'm waiting for the water.

A few weeks after this new pattern developed, Tom discovered her alternate home, a nest in the hayloft where she had formed a warm, round, cozy hollow in a back corner between some hay bales.

As the days got progressively colder, we seldom saw Elf at the house. I snuck several times into the barn to where I could observe her. Raccoons do not hibernate, but when the temperature is around 20 degrees or colder they stay in their nest in a sort of drowsy sleep. Elf was asleep most of the time. When she wasn't she would be idly playing with her fingers or rolling a piece of hay between her paws contentedly passing the long, cold winter.

The breeding season of raccoons is during late January, February or early March. We didn't know if Elf would accept a mate because of her human upbringing. Orphans are generally "slower" in such matters because of the lack of many skills only a wild mother could teach.

In February, several neighbors stopped to see us and teasingly ask if we'd taught Elf the "facts of life" or talked to her about the "birds and the bees." They were sure it was Elf they'd seen up on the hill with another raccoon. Reports of "side by side", "nose to nose" and "kissing" raccoons were being brought to us.

The male raccoon stays only a week or so with his chosen female and then moves on. The gestation period is 63 to 64 days. The female raises two to seven kits, with four young as the average.

We still didn't see much of Elf. When we did it was still almost impossible to determine if she was pregnant. Pregnancy can be difficult to determine because raccoons are round, pudgy, roly-poly, with hide enough for two. They have so much extra skin that if you grasp an adult by the nape of the neck, he can literally roll over completely and wrap his legs about the arm that is still holding firmly to its neck.

We who handle raccoons quickly learn to respect their tremendously strong jaw muscles which they use to rip and tear. Their teeth are actually quite blunt, but if they bite they may break the skin. In most cases your finger will feel more as if it were squeezed by a vice.

By the middle of April,we knew Elf had become a mother, because she began to chase the men from the barn. You had to be very sure she was occupied in the hayloft with her kits if you wanted to enter the barn. If she was not, you left in a hurry, driven by an enraged raccoon snapping at your ankles.

Where's the water for my bath?

When Elf came to the house for food and drink, she was her old mischievous self. We now had a raccoon trapped in two worlds, thanks to human intervention. Elf looked on us as her parents and protectors, but since she herself became a parent, all her deeply rooted instincts warned her that we represented danger.

At four weeks of age, the kits' eyes opened and two weeks later they were strong enough to follow their mother for short distances. Before those six weeks expired, we located a hollow tree with a cavity the right size and an access hole the right diameter and height from the ground. For six weeks we adjusted our schedule to fit Elf's and tried to comfort her in her confusion.

Moving day arrived. While Elf was at the nearby brook I quickly got her four extremely chubby kits into a cage. As the last of the four was being shut in, Elf arrived at the barn door. As I expected, she had heard

Racoon etiquette at mealtime.

Is it time to eat yet?

them screaming with fear. What I didn't expect was to look down and see a hundred-pound Elf. All her fur was on end, which made her seem double in size; her lips were drawn back and her teeth were gleaming. This was coupled with the most menacing growl for an animal that size! I knew beforehand that the situation I was putting myself in held a certain amount of danger. If Elf had been a bear confronting a cub-knapper, my hair couldn't have stood up any straighter.

As I kept my eyes squarely on Elf, and leaving the cage with the kits securely locked inside, I moved across the haymow to the top of the ladder. Spitting and growling, Elf positioned herself at the foot of the ladder. We both waited as the kits continued their screams of panic. After several minutes, I decided to end the stand-off and quietly started down the ladder. When I was half-way down, Elf rushed the ladder, still in a fury. As she came hurtling up, I jumped and was already running before I hit the floor. I sprinted for the house, but Elf caught me half-way and nipped at my heels the rest of the way to the door. While this was going on, Tom raced up the ladder, grabbed the cage full of kits and raced back down the ladder in double-time. He left the cage on the barn floor and exited through the barn's back door. He made it to the house unmolested.

We now waited for Elf to have time to realize that the kits were un-harmed, although unreachable. A half-hour later, we entered the barn wearing work boots and welding gloves. Tom carried another cage for Elf, while I lugged the food she might require until she was familiar with her new environment.

Elf lay by the cage with her paws reaching inside to caress her babies. Upon seeing us, she stood with hackles raised, but in her eyes and face all we saw was total confusion.

Tom quickly grabbed her by the nape of the neck and then her tail. Before she could begin to retaliate, she was caged. We then wired the two cages together. I gathered up the food and we set off for the new home we'd selected for Elf and her young ones.

At the tree, we placed the babies carefully inside and then held Elf's cage up to the opening and tumbled her in. I placed the food a few feet from the tree, between it and the brook, and then we quickly retreated.

Twenty-four hours later I returned, no closer than necessary, to ob-serve. Elf and the kits were in the brook some distance upstream. I left more food before leaving and every other day for two weeks I brought food, until one day not all of the food was gone. Thereafter, I brought no food, fearing it might attract other animals. We checked the tree once in a while throughout that summer. There were baby raccoon prints as well as Elf's, all up and down the brook. By fall, there were very few signs of them, and in late fall we checked the tree and it was empty.

Every fall, as each new orphan goes its own way, I find myself on the verge of tears. Then I remind myself that this moment is in fact what I have strived for since they came to me. So I go home, shoulder-ing a mixture of sadness and elation. But the time with Elf reconfirms the reality that wild animals cannot forever remain tame.

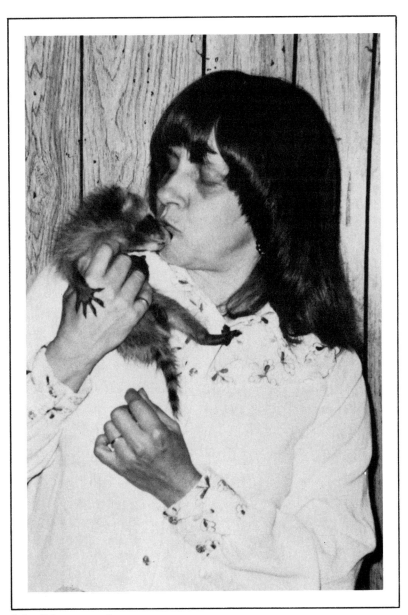

I don't have a mother.

Tzari in her "hunter orange."

Chapter 3
Week-o's Story

Week-o's story begins as have those of most of the orphans: a phone call from a worried human referred by the local animal shelter to me. The caller was having a house built overlooking a small private pond. A Canada goose had limped her way up the hill from the water and settled down near the foundation of the house. The presence of neither humans nor a dog deterred her from staying.

A friend, Christine, and I set out to rescue her, taking with us a blanket to throw over her and a big box to hold her in. Geese can give a fierce pinch with their beaks, resulting in a bruise which you feel acutely for several days.

Our game plan was to keep the goose interested in one of us while the other snuck up behind her and threw the blanket completely over the bird.

I kept the goose distracted as Christine did the sneaking and blanket-tossing. The blanket in place over the bird, Christine picked up the goose and held it tightly. Within seconds the goose had pushed and wiggled her head free, but instead of hissing and biting, she rubbed the side of her head against Christine's arm, calling softly "Week-o" "Week-o". The goose was tame. Because of that soft, incessant call, we named her Week-o.

I learned later that it's not uncommon for some people to net a new-born goose from the water as it paddles along behind its mother. They

38

often keep the goose penned for a while as a pet, but soon tire of it, usually in late summer when it's perhaps three months old. By this time, it weighs 8 to 12 pounds and is extremely messy. The convenient solution is to set the bird free. People feel there is no harm done, though in fact the potential for damage is great. The released goose is treated as an outcast by its kin and so can find no safety in numbers. Moreover, it has no idea of how to forage on its own and is almost utterly ignorant of its natural, wild enemies. The bird also had no flight training and does not have the strength to keep up with the flock when it is time to move south and falls by the wayside.

Week-o showed us with nuzzling affection how pleased she was to be in a human's arms again. We placed her in the big box and headed home to the oft-repeated sounds of "Week-o, Week-o," at times soft and trilling, at others, a more strident call.

At home, we placed her on the ground to watch her walk. Her left foot appeared to be so sore that she could hardly place it on the ground. Tom and I examined the foot and could find no sign of injury, past or present.

I placed a phone call to the veterinarians at the Little River Veterinarian Hospital and made an appointment for Week-o to be brought in the following day for x-rays.

I took Week-o up late the next day as she would have to spend the night. That evening, the doctors would sedate her to enable them to x-ray a motionless leg and foot: geese don't like to have people playing with their feet and legs. I came home and tried not to worry. Birds do not take anesthesia well.

The next morning I fairly raced to the hospital. As I entered, I met a group of smiling faces, including Week-o's. Doctor George Holmes and Doctor Tricia Rose told me how they had found two widely divergent dose recommendations. To solve the dilemma, they started with the least amount and after some time, added a bit more until Week-o was sedated.

At first, Week-o was just rubbing her cheek against Tricia's, but as she became drowsier she tried to wrap her long, elegant neck completely around Tricia's, all the while softly calling "Week-o, Week-o". The wild babies love and respect their immediate human family but the rule of the wild—'All strangers are suspect''—can make the veterinarians' work hazardous. I breathed a sigh of relief, glad to know that another one of my wildlife orphans had been on its best behavior.

The x-rays revealed absolutely nothing. The severe limp was either a sprain or a congenital defect. The diagnosis was to keep her on the ground; no floating about a pond. If it was a sprain, walking would eventually get the foot back in action. If it were congenital, she would never get better. Time would give us the answer.

Geese cannot become airborne without getting a running start. If Week-o's foot was not properly functional, she would never fly.

When Week-o and I got home, she followed me around as I caught up on the chores. I then proceeded to build her a pen out of chicken wire. She would need to be penned so that when one of us couldn't be around she would be safe from traffic and anything else she could think of to get into.

After a long afternoon of driving in fence posts and stringing up the chicken wire, making sure it firmly hugged the ground and stood at least four feet high, I was ready for a rest. Instead, Week-o and I went into the house, I to fix supper and she to float for an hour or so in the bathtub. We ate supper to the soft and trilling accompaniment of "Week-o," "Week-o."

Week-o was a perfect lady in the tub. Humans have been known to splash more water about and have left a dirtier bathtub ring.

When I lifted the bathtub handle to let the water run out, Week-o immediately realized that the water level was dropping. In less time than it takes to talk about it, she had discovered where the drain was. She attempted to stop the flow with her beak, then her webbed feet. She might have used her body except it was too buoyant. I left her to her contortions and the diminishing water supply while I quickly did the dishes. When I went to fetch Week-o, the tub had drained dry despite her valiant efforts, but she was happily preening away at her feathers. When I picked her up, she was practically dry.

Week-o followed us to the barn and watched with great interest as we brought in the horses and cows to feed them. She limped along after us as we did the rest of the evening chores and seemed to enjoy herself immensely. As the outside pen would not be secure against predators who would have the dark and time to help broach the chicken-wire pen, we closed Week-o up for the night in the hen building.

Early the next morning, as we came outdoors, we heard Week-o trilling for us. We released her and again she accompanied us on our round of chores.

After another 48 hours had passed, it was obvious that Week-o had elected herself official chore-helper.

The following weekend, when my friend Sog and I built a fence for another horse pasture, our work was lightened by Week-o's antics. She watched us with critically alert eye. As each strand of electric wire was run from an insulator on one fence post to the insulator on the next, Week-o reached up and pulled the wire with her beak as if to test its tautness. She would then draw herself up to her full height, honk softly and limp to the next fence post, waiting patiently there for us to run the wire down to her. Later that day, we led the horses to their lush green pasture, Week-o following closely behind. The animals made a picture that I will see in my mind's eye for the rest of my life. A handsome, grey Appaloosa gelding with black leopard spots dappling his rump, followed closely by a prancing Arab-Quarter horse mare, her bay coat glistening in the sun. Limping along, bringing up the rear, was the Canada goose in her gorgeous plummage.

The horses stopped only long enough to grab a quick mouthful of

A first snow gallop.

grass, then were off at a gallop, following the fence-line of their new pasture. Week-o caught the air of excitement and began limping rapidly up and down one side of the fence line, hooting. As the horses went galloping past, Week-o reached up and tugged on the electric fence wire. With a startled honk and a furious, feathery shake, she immediately let go of the wire. After sticking her offended tongue out several times and repeatedly honking at the pernicious wire, she reached up and grabbed the wire again; more ruffling of feathers, startled hooting and running her tongue in and out. This time, she eyed the wire thoughtfully. Slowly and reflectively, she proceeded to limp down the fence line, all the while eyeing the wire. Never again did she touch the wire with her beak unless she saw one of us handle the wire first.

As summer days lingered longer with increased daylight, our farm life was in high gear with the added chores of helping the assorted wildlife become more self-sufficient, getting in the hay, spreading manure and hauling out treelength logs from the woodlot to be cut up in the fall and used as firewood during the coming winter. It was easy to lose track of Week-o in the bustle. One always assumed and hoped that she was "helping" one of us. The only times she was penned were at nighttime or when the mowing machine was in use cutting the grass.

One early afternoon, I discovered that the human residents of our bailiwik were all accounted for, but not Week-o. An hour earlier I had put her in the chicken-wire enclosure because the horses were being shod and I didn't want her in the way. I proceeded to check the barn and surrounding pasture while Tom went to the hayfield to help our neighbor, Paul, load hay onto a wagon pulled by his matched pair of work ponies.

Tom came back shortly, lugging a goose. Harried, I asked him, "Have you found Week-o?" "If this isn't Week-o," he answered, "we now have two geese." It was Week-o, but it wasn't far-fetched to think it might have been another goose. We have had other young wildlife drift in with those that we already have.

Paul and his young sons, it turned out, had been loading the hay when son P.J. called to his father on the opposite side of the wagon that he had a goose helping him.

"Yep," said Paul.

"But Dad," P.J. said, "it's a Canada goose. It belongs on a pond, not in a hayfield."

"Yep," said Paul.

Paul, like most of our neighbors, was accustomed to finding most any kind of wildlife popping up about his feet when visiting our farm. Before Paul got around to explaining, Tom had appeared, scooped Week-o up in his arms and headed back to the house, two small boys watching with mouths agape.

As soon as the horses were shod and the farrier had left, Week-o and I went to examine her chicken-wire enclosure in an effort to discover how she had escaped. I had built her a fairly large pen but I thought I had made it short enough so that, if she became capable of flight, she wouldn't have runway enough to gain the altitude needed to fly out. The fence was tight to the ground so she couldn't slip beneath it. Everything looked okay. I couldn't figure it out. Week-o wasn't talking. Her limp was getting better, but we hadn't seen her attempt to fly. To this day, we haven't solved the mystery.

The next day our neighbor, Wayne, came down on his tractor, towing his woods trailer on which Tom was to do some welding. Week-o showed more than a passing interest in the machine. She appeared to be attracted to the sound of the engine and addressed it with honking. After a few minutes of talk with Tom, Wayne was back on his tractor and roaring off up the road.

Suddenly, Week-o's feet were slapping down the driveway after him. Take-off! She positioned herself beside Wayne's left shoulder, flying in formation with him. She then uttered the most joyous "HONK!" we'd ever heard. Wayne's head did a classic double-take as the tractor veered sharply to the right. Wayne brought himself and the tractor under control and came to a quick stop. Week-o's landing wasn't the most graceful in goosedom, but she was so thrilled with her accomplishment that the bumbled landing didn't seem to bother her a bit.

After getting Week-o under control and back on her home ground in one piece, we relaxed enough to enjoy the humor of it all. Week-o obviously would be able some day to lead a normal life, but she couldn't be allowed to fly south this year because she simply wouldn't have the strength, nor the companions.

I specialize in mammals, but many volunteer wildlife rehabilitators specialize in birds and I needed the counsel of just such an expert, one especially knowledgeable in the ways of geese.

The next day, with the Camden Animal Shelter's gracious help, we located a new home for Week-o, the Stanwood Wildlife Foundation in Ellsworth, better known as "Birdsacre". A wildlife sanctuary and a wild-life recovery center, Birdsacre is run by Mr. Richmond, who informed us that they had four Canada geese at that time, three of which were permanently injured. The fourth was on the road to a complete recovery. To Week-o's potential benefit, it was a young male. Besides having a flock of geese for company, she and the young male might pair off in a relationship that among their kind is life-long.

I planned to take Week-o to Birdsacre the next day, before she could get into real trouble with her new-found abilities. But that afternoon Week-o was escorting Tom when they heard a motorcycle approaching. Week-o was off and running. Almost instantly she was flying leftshoul-der formation, as she had with Wayne, beside the unknown motorcy-clist. I'll give the guy credit for having nerves of steel: the bike hardly swerved as Week-o gave her joyous "HONK!" and settled in just off his shoulder for what was fast becoming her classic flight formation. But I can picture the startled motorcyclist's face behind the full face guard, eyes as big as dinner-plates! The motorcyclist slowed down, and either the reduction in his speed or Tom's insistent whistle encouraged Week-o to bank sharply to the left, bringing her back to her own door-yard. Our unknown motorcyclist kept right on going. I wonder if any-one believed his story ... if he saw fit to tell it.

"Tomorrow" came. Christine, Week-o in her travel cage, and I be-gan the long drive to Ellsworth. Week-o seemed to enjoy the passing scenery. When we at last crossed the Bucksport bridge, Week-o showed her excitement with considerable tail wagging, feather rustling and trill-ing. Christine and I decided she had been aroused by the smell of the tidal river.

Upon arriving at Birdsacre we were greeted by Mr. Richmond. We took Week-o to the goose enclosure and I released her from her cage. The other geese were ready and willing to greet her. Alas, Week-o took one look at these strange birds and gave a loud, distressing cry that rose almost to a screech. She hurled her body into me, wrapped her long, elegant neck about mine, rapidly rubbed her cheek against my face and whimpered softly and incessantly, "week-o... week-o ..." I looked up at Mr. Richmond. He removed his pipe from his mouth and with a soft, understanding smile said, "She'll be all right. It takes time, especially if they're human-imprinted."

Week-O enjoying her bathtub swim.

We left Week-o to get acquainted with her new environment as Mr. Richmond gave us a tour of his facilities, where he has every species of owl indigenous to the state of Maine. The owls on display are permanently crippled, with no hope of rehabilitation. My favorites were the little saw-whets owls. Perhaps some day I will have the opportunity to raise a saw-whet. The larger owls require such specialized knowledge and attention that unless I had a near-by rehabilitator to tutor me I could not properly raise one. In fact, my ignorance could easily kill such a bird.

After Mr. Richmond had taken us through his facilities and spent much more time with us than he probably had to spare, he took us to a building that overlooked Week-o and her new friends. They hadn't quite become friends yet. Every few minutes, Week-o would dash about looking for us, but it brightened my day to see she was at least talking to her new associates.

I am glad that I have complete confidence in Mr. Richmond's ability as a rehabilitator for any decisions concerning Week-o are now his.

We said good-bye to Mr. Richmond, and a silent good-bye to a very special goose.

Springtime, two years later, I received a note from Mr. Richmond that Week-o had flown south that preceding fall with a group of Canada geese and had just returned to Bridsacre with the spring.

Each spring and fall as the Canada geese fly overhead, my heart skips a beat as I hear their calls and I softly whisper ''Week-o''.

Sweet Pea and Little Bit go exploring.

Chapter 4
Sweet Pea and Me

My introduction to the striped skunk, a member of the Mustelidae or weasel family, began on a warm, calm day in June. After receiving the usual phone call of a plea for assistance and getting directions to the site of this newest waif, I was on my way. On a street in Camden, I found one very small, vividly black and white skunk wandering around the base of an oak tree. He did indeed give the impression of being lost and acted decidedly dejected. Scouting about the area, I looked for his mother or siblings. Finding neither, I returned to the oak tree, sat on the ground near the little fellow and began to talk softly to him. Within seconds he was snuggling between my bent legs, nuzzling and murmuring. I scooped him up slowly and gently. He wriggled contentedly in the palm of my hand. I fed him a teaspoon of glucose from a plastic hypodermic syringe without the needle which he accepted greedily and happily. I found his teeth were just beginning to erupt from his gums. His eyes had barely become fully opened and his sex was male. I was surprised to find that his little body smelled as fresh and clean as a new-mown lawn. Like all babies with a contented stomach, he became sleepy and curled up into my palm. I slid him gently into the top pocket of my bib-overalls, where he fit perfectly!

Soon after returning home I offered him a half-spoonful of canned dog food moistened with some cow's milk in a saucer. He waded into it, literally.

Holding baby by nape of the neck.

In the meantime, I sat on the floor, making myself as comfortable as possible while awaiting further developments. After he had finished eating, the skunk waddled about, exploring his new environment. Watching him waddle away from me, I noticed he was very "low-posted" to the ground, hind-end higher and broader than the front, the inside of the hind legs wide apart and forming a square exactly the shape of a staple. Now I understand why I had never seen a skunk do much more than waddle about. When pressed to the extreme, they can break into a remarkable smooth gallop, but skunks have little need to run from their foes.

Seeing me watching him, he arched and flattened his tail so that it laid tightly against his spine. He stamped his feet while his toenails tap-danced a warning on my linoleum! He tap-danced and bounced his body toward me, then slid backwards half his length, toenails dragging on the floor. I never moved, but I could feel my whole body demanding to run, faint, do anything but engage in a stand-off with what appeared to be a perturbed and well-armed skunk. My mind was arguing intent-ly with my body, repeating over and over, "This is a baby; he's harm-less. Babies play by emulating the behavior of their parents."

Again, he repeated his toe-tapping bounce, only this time not only did his eyes face me but so did his rump! This little guy was hinged in the middle! With his tail held tightly against his back, he gave the appearance of having three eyes, two small and black; one round and pink. The pink eye gave me the distinct feeling that I was looking down the wrong end of a very small but extremely powerful double-barreled shotgun. My heart ceased beating.

This is my favorite toy.

Smile for the camera.

Seconds later, he was clawing at my legs and rolling around, romping about with the agility of a kitten. I resumed breathing!

A skunk has two "scent" glands, one on each side of the anus. An adult can spray more than 20 feet in a favorable wind. At six feet, the spray is so precise that the sprayed area can be covered with a quarter. The spray is a sulfur-alcohol compound which can cause intense eye pain and a sore throat from breathing the fumes. There are a few unsubstantiated reports of permanent blindness.

As I picked myself up from the floor, still somewhat giddy, he went back to exploring his foreign surroundings, shuffling about with purposeful curiosity.

I proceeded to catch up on some kitchen chores. As I opened a cupboard door, the tap dancing began anew. I found myself freezing in place and immediately assumed my dual personality again, my body demanding motion or cardiac arrest, my mind commanding stoic motionlessness. A century at least—an eon perhaps—seemed to pass before the skunk was perched on my foot, scratching with his unbelievably long claws into the edges of my sneaker. The long, curved, bear-like claws on a skunk's front feet are designed for digging up grubs and earthworms, but they can be very effective sneaker-shredders.

Tom arrived home to find our "first-ever" baby skunk. Within minutes the little skunk put Tom through the same ritual I had endured.

Dynamite enjoying her dinner.

Dynamite fascinated by moving water.

I think Tom was more uncomfortable than I had been but he's a very logical person. Skunks have only one defense. The little guy acted as if he felt he was in danger. Tom worried, as well he might, about the logical conclusion.

I went to prepare supper, leaving the two of them to work out an acquaintance. The skunk was alternating between tap dancing and cuddling Tom's foot.

I busied myself with the cooking, thinking that if anything went amiss I'd certainly smell it first, We operate on the theory that proceeding calmly and routinely helps the orphans to settle down and feel protected. In the past this had worked. Will it work for a skunk?

When I looked to see how things were progressing, I found a very contented baby skunk curled up, fast asleep, in the crook of Tom's arm as he serenely read the paper.

Just as supper was about to be served, Tom started chuckling. The little skunk's nose, it seems, had been snuffling the good food smells even while he was asleep. His eyes flew open and his entire body was wriggling with anticipation. Laughing, Tom placed him gently on the floor. As Tom walked to the kitchen, a very hungry skunk was bouncing along behind him. Tom dubbed him "Sweet-Pea" then and there.

Tom dished him up a bit of mashed potato, string beans and finely chopped meat. Sweet-Pea waded in with gusto.

While we ate our supper, Sweet-Pea re-explored his new surroundings, but in an extremely relaxed mood, as indicated by his drooping tail, its tip almost brushing the floor.

When we finished our supper, our border collie Jewel scratched at the kitchen door, telling us it was time for her supper. As I went to let her in, Tom and I mentally girded ourself for another test.

Ilet Jewel in and put down her supper. Sweet-Pea watched, wide-eyed and alert, from the other side of the kitchen. Soon, the smell of more food and the sound of Jewel's enjoyment of it became too much and he waddled over to the dish. They eyed each other for a moment, then Sweet-Pea lifted his tail on high, stamped his feet and presented his rump to the dog. Undeterred, Jewel resumed eating, whereupon the little skunk bellied up to the dish and joined her. Jewel willingly gave him a corner but let him know with a growl the rest was off-limits! Sweet-Pea accepted the terms and Tom and I breathed a sigh of relief.

A few minutes later, Jewel was curled up in her favorite corner behind the wood stove and Sweet-Pea was wriggling contentedly against her belly.

Since I have volunteered to be a wildlife rehabilitator, we have had several dogs. Regardless of the sex or breed of the dogs, they have all shared their home and food and have given protection and the warmth of their bodies if the orphans desired it.

I worried at first that the orphans might unknowingly accept as a friend and ally another dog that might find its way onto our land, but nature's rule of "trust family but flee from outsiders" held true.

Sweet Pea snuggling with Jewel.

Within a few days, Sweet-Pea had the household routine well in hand. He knew his meals were served four times a day. He knew where the door to the outside was. He became very busy trying to make friends with all the other inhabitants of the farm.

The foxes found him too slow-of-foot to be any fun. They were intrigued at first by his industrious digging of shallow holes in the lawn but found his taste for worms and grubs definitely beneath their taste.

Our Siamese cat was under the impression that she had been supplanted by a kitten. But her haughtiness was replaced by downright indignation when she finally allowed herself to examine his body closely. She never again admitted he existed.

The raccoons, being not much bigger at that time than Sweet-Pea, accepted him as a somewhat retarded brother. Sweet-Pea could play with them, keep up with their ambling walk if he really hustled, but he flunked at playing in the water and showed no interest at all in climbing!

The horses were friendly enough but were too tall to communicate with easily.

The Canada goose, Week-o, rather enjoyed grub-hunting with him but she was quicker than he and evidently he felt she got more than her share of the menu. So Sweet-Pea decided to become an escort of humans. He did quite well, except for the fact he couldn't decide whether to lead or follow, so he opted for navigating between one's legs. We were continually tripping over the little fellow. Besides not wanting to injure him, we were concerned about setting off that effective shotgun of his.

Several days after Sweet-Pea's arrival, we discovered facts about the firing mechanism of that weapon.

Tom and I had decided that the day had arrived when our combination storehouse and horse-barn had to have its annual cleaning. As we worked at resorting, stacking and, the hardest part of all, throwing away the accumulation, the animals slowly congregated. Week-o was first on the scene since she had assumed the role of primary chore girl and was never far from our side. Sweet-Pea joined us after making his grub-rounds on the lawn.

We found ourselves continually zig-zagging around the goose who, as we went by, insisted on reaching up with that long neck of hers, trying to grab whatever we had in our arms. At the same time, we were trying to keep an eye on Sweet-Pea, who may or may not have been beneath our feet. Within minutes, three raccoons had entered the fracas. They wished to help us, too. After all, they had hands. Between the raccoons merrily moving and examining objects, the goose trying to pluck those same objects from our arms after we'd wrestled them from the raccoons and Sweet-Pea bouncing along somewhere between our feet, the situation was fast becoming the proverbial zoo!

Fortunately, the animals soon tired of the game. Week-o returned to the lawn. Sweet-Pea and the raccoons decided to play among themselves at the farther end of the barn.

Tom and I were at last making some headway when we heard distinct highpitched weasel screams.

Sweet-Pea was being used as a pull toy. One raccoon was pulling him forward while the other had a grip on his tail and was pulling him backward. When they released Sweet-Pea, he was so angry that he was actually vibrating up and down, simultaneously stamping his feet and squealing. The raccoons were overjoyed. They were rubbing their paws with glee, their eyes sparkling with merriment. Their mildly retarded friend was entertaining after all. As soon as Sweet-Pea started to settle down, they double-teamed him again. When he started to squeal, they again released him and waited avidly for the bouncing and stamping. They were not disappointed!

Tom and I were fairly sure that Sweet-Pea was not being hurt, but his pride was taking a beating. We were astonished and relieved that Sweet-Pea hadn't sprayed, especially in the barn. But we were puzzled. Why didn't he retaliate? Was he too young? Was there a physical problem?

As round four started, we smelled skunk for the first time since Sweet-Pea had arrived. The air was thick with it. The raccoon that had grabbed Sweet-Pea by the tail was sitting back on his haunches with a very puzzled look on his face.

Tom and I left the barn for some fresh air. Shortly, we were joined by Sweet-Pea who was again his familiar, sweet-natured self. Well, not quite. As Tom picked him up, he noticed just the faintest smell of skunk. When the raccoons emerged from the barn, I picked up the one who

Dynamite proving she's really a pussycat.

was on the receiving end of Sweet-Pea's wrath and was amazed to find hardly any odor.

Thinking that somehow Sweet-Pea must have missed his target, we re-entered the barn to investigate the situation. There was no hint of skunk smell. We knew what we had seen and remembered acutely what we had smelled. We were stumped. Skunk spray is supposed to be practically indestructible. It's good for weeks! What had happened here?

Over the next few months we "riddled it out" and the answer has stood the test of time. Skunks have two distinct ways of defending themselves. The one we all know and dread to encounter is the classic spray, a jet of the sulfur-alcohol compound. It has astonishing penetration and the odor remains active for 60 days if not treated.

The second type of spray appears to consist of a release of the gas by itself without accompanying liquid. The gas mixes with the oxygen in the air and although the smell itself is as noxious as the liquid spray, it completely dissipates within a few minutes. This explains how one can be awakened at night by a stiff skunk smell and yet five minutes later be unable to detect the animal. This ability to release a gas-only deterrent is an advantage for the skunk. A skunk can spray several times, each jet of the anal gland oil using about a fifth of a tablespoon. Because each gland must replenish itself sooner or later with liquid, this enables the skunk to first release the gaseous odor, following if necessary with the liquid spray. For the person or animal crossing the skunk's path, this warning is also of great advantage.

We have come to know and love the striped skunk. It is an intelligent animal, as playful as a roomful of kittens and as immaculate as the cat. Hopefully, all states will outlaw the surgical de-scenting of skunks as this exceptional mechanism is truly their only defense used only when they feel their life is in grave and imminent danger. Skunks are fantastic mousers and eat many grubs and insects that are harmful to farmers' crops and backyard gardens alike.

Sweet-Pea bounced through his childhood on the farm. As summer wore on, he adopted a portion of the space under the barn as his own. Only once, that we know of, did he spray: one of the foxes was playfully practicing his hunting skills on Sweet-Pea and the game must have become too rough; Sweet-Pea let him have it. The young fox wore his scented badge of "honor" on his chest for several weeks.

For a while, Sweet-Pea continued to arrive regularly for morning and evening feedings, but quite often we saw him hunting about our fields and pastures. As fall came, we saw him less and less. He was learning that the best hunting times are the dark hours of dusk to dawn. As further evidence of his independence, he had established a new home in an old woodchuck burrow by the far edge of the cow pasture.

It is very rare for a rehabilitator to be able to continue to watch an orphan that has adapted to the wild. Once they have returned to their natural world, they become as elusive as any wildborn. This time, I was lucky to observe that Sweet-Pea was successful in his own world.

3

1

5

I love a snack.

Salt and Pepper. Or, Pepper and Salt?

Sweet Pea celebrating Christmas.

Chapter 5
Prickles The Porcupine

Prickles was only a few weeks old when we first saw him on a mid-May morning. He was sitting in a mud puddle on a dirt road, looking wet and miserable and moaning lustily when human hands scooped him up to bring him home.

He was about five inches long and weighed only about one pound. His quills were a quarter-inch long and the thickness of a very fine needle. Porcupettes are born with their quills. The fetus is encased in a protective and nutritive embryo sac which bursts at birth. Within a half-hour, their once-supple little quills have hardened and the porcupette has 30,000 reasons to be respected. If startled, the porcupine immediately buries its head, turns its body toward the intruder and flails away with its tail.

I wore welding gloves when feeding Prickles. He consumed 1 teaspoon of special formula every three hours throughout the day. I did not feed him through the night.

Within a few days, he was convinced that I was mama and after each feeding he tried to crawl into the crook of my arm and cuddle. Having removed a quill or two from the welding gloves after each feeding, I was somewhat apprehensive about this display of affection, but I decided to take appropriate precautions and see what happened.

At the next feeding, I wore several heavy shirts and willed myself into absolute calm and confidence. Prickles crawled slowly up and off the welding glove to nestle in the bend of my arm. Porcupines make a sur-

Porcupines prowl around the ground.

prising range of sounds. Unprickeled I listened to his sounds of contentment and security and enjoyed our mutual sense of trust.

Once we became fully acquainted, I discarded the welding gloves. Porcupines do not have quills on their legs or on the underparts of their bodies. Their fur in these places is long and soft, and their warm, round bellies are a joy to hold. When removing Prickles from his cage I would place my hand palm up so he could crawl onto my hand. He would clutch my wrist like a tree limb and I would lift him to the table where he would sit up, keeping his front paws on one of my hands for balance while he greedily suckled the formula held in my other hand.

Prickles loved to be stroked and tickled; but one had to respect the lay of his quills and not rub against the "grain." The quills are so sharp that just touching the end of one lightly can leave it firmly implanted in your skin. It requires a good tug to remove one and it smarts! I prefer not to know how it feels to have the quills driven in by a quick slap of the tail.

Porcupines love to climb.

A quill is designed with microscopic barbs on the end. The quill itself is a hollow shaft, sealed at both ends. When a quill enters the flesh, the movement of the victim's muscles pulls the quill deeper. Amazingly—and gruesomely - the quills will move internally throughout an animal's body, turning only when meeting bone. It is possible for quills to puncture any internal organ.

Within a few days of her arrival, Prickles was sampling a variety of foods. His favorites were cauliflower, apples and tender branch tips of maple, willow and aspen.

His formula and the company of humans were his priorities. He was almost always "moaning" for us to pick him up and cuddle. He seemed to feel he was the most adorable, cuddly porcupette on mother nature's earth.

If company was gathered around the table at his feeding time, Prickles, after eating his own meal, gleefully waddled around to greet each and every human. If a guest smelled especially interesting, he would attempt to climb into his or her arms! This was invariable met with trepidation on the part of our visitors.

Nonetheless, a surprising number of people were ultimately willing to try holding a procupette. It required only a few simple instructions and a do-or-die promise on my part to immediately rescue said human if necessary. And a measure of faith.

Porcupettes must eventually grow up and become porcupines, so more serious events were planned by us to prepare Prickles for that inevitability. A tall, narrow cage was built and furnished with the top part of an aspen tree. Lessons in tree climbing and bark-eating were utmost in our minds. Monkeys are famous for hanging from a limb with their front paws and swinging up onto that limb with their hind legs. Prickles did the same, but he did it so-o much slower!

While I was busy supplying fresh leaves and branches daily, Prickles nibbled bark, chewed leaves into green slimy pulp, played, slept and drank his formula out of a dish.

In a few more weeks I planned to release Prickles. I had a grove of spruce and fir picked out for him, one with a porcupine family in the nearby area and the grove itself close enough for me to check-up on him occasionally.

A year hence, Prickles would look for a mate. Because of a porcupine's equipment, it's natural for people to question the feasibility of porcupines mating. When a female accepts a male, she simply raises her tail over her back. The rest is typically mammalian. Gestation takes about 209 days and the babies are born as early as April, as late as June. Usually, a single young is born.

Prickles died in June. This is when a rehabilitator can easily become a depressed, irrational person. You reexamine, minutely, every food introduced to this animal and its effect on the body system. You have watched the health of the coat, the brightness of the eyes and the rate of growth. Prickles had been growing, but not nearly as well as he

Hiding.

should. The cause of his death was never determined.

A small percentage of wild animals are abandoned by their mothers because they are physically or mentally impaired. To human eyes, these babies may seem perfectly fit. When an animal arrives in the care of a rehabilitator obviously injured or sick, the potential for its death must be accepted. The deaths of apparently healthy animals like Prickles can maim a rehabilitator's confidence.

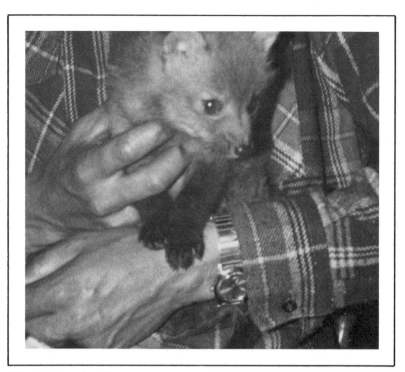

Kit only 4 weeks old.

Kit reaches 5 weeks old.

Chapter 6
Curious Kit

On a warm April afternoon, the Warden Service rescued a very small, bedraggled fox that had been sitting alone in a marsh. Some boys had spotted him and one went to fetch the warden.

The fox was about one month old. He was so small that when he was curled up asleep, he fit in the palm of my hand. His eyes were blue, and he had blacktipped ears and a black nose. His legs below the joints were black. His body hair was fawn-colored, with a hint of German-Shepherd puppy grey with black guard hairs. His face showed faint signs of the red to come. He could easily be mistaken for a puppy unless you observed his tail closely: the hair was short, dense and bushy and the tail as a whole was nearly cylindrical.

Red foxes mate in late January and the female delivers in March after a gestation period of about 53 days. The young are called kits or pups and the typical litter numbers from four to six. Both parents care for their young for the first eight to 10 days, the male bringing food to the female. As the kits become older, both parents will bring food to the den for themselves and the kits. The kits are dark brown at birth, weighing approximately three and a half ounces. Their eyes open when they are eight to 10 days old. At one month of age, they occasionally peek out of the opening of their den. At about six weeks, they begin to play outside and at two months they start following their parents abroad to learn the techniques of hunting. By the end of October, the kits begin dispersing to establish their own territories. If the food supply is sufficient, they will have a home range of one square mile, rarely more than four miles.

The diet for our fox, unimaginatively but appropriately named Kit, was simple: a little milk and canned dog food. The little guy made himself a member of the family at once. He ate, quietly explored his new environment and curled up with the dog.

After a busy evening of getting all the orphans settled down for the night, Kit, too, was asleep by the kitchen stove; I turned out the lights and headed up to bed. My head had barely touched the pillow when Kit let out a howl. No warning, no preamble. It was just there, starting at the top of the scale and quavering down. The hair on the back of my neck stood upright. Another howl. For the sake of sanity and a good night's sleep, I reluctantly fetched him into our bed. Kit immediately snuggled down between Tom and me and the night slipped by quietly.

Tom's early-rising schedule suited Kit perfectly. Tom took the fox and the dog downstairs with him and put them immediately outside. Kit followed the dog's lead and did his duty. Tom then brought them back in for their breakfast.

Although Tom grumbled to our friends about how crowded the bed was getting, it was evident that he was completely bewitched by this small ball of fur. We all were. Kit was every inch the young gentleman. He was quiet, immaculate and on his way to being completely house-broken. Within 48 hours of his arrival, he knew his feeding times and the location of his dish. He also quickly learned to beg for more milk by sitting in front of the refrigerator.

For all of Kit's progress and disarming character, I began to notice that he never responded to his name or a whistle. The only times he came when he was called, were while he was facing the caller and making direct eye contact. Was Kit deaf?

It's difficult to test an animal that is born deaf. They are so attuned to using air vibrations set off by noise that they will respond much as hearing animals do, to loud noises, such as the slamming of a door, a gunshot or a dog's sharp bark. These and other noise-producing events make air turbulance, which is picked up as sensory vibrations by the deaf.

For our own test, I held Kit while Tom came quietly up behind us and brought his hands together in a sharp clap behind Kit's head. The sound elicited no response from Kit. Let the dog give a warning bark and Kit would respond by immediately hiding under the couch. Did he see the dog's agitation? Pick up air waves? Was he just hearing impaired and not utterly deaf? We placed Kit in a tall, roomy box for short periods of time until he accepted this as a normal part of his routine. Then we made all kinds of noises; hand claps, whistles, pots banging, doors slamming. The verdict was still unclear but in our judgment Kit was, at the least, hearing impaired.

Had Kit been abandoned by his parents because he was physically unfit for life in the wild? To humans this may sound exceptionally cruel, but still-nursing young animals that are abandoned will become cold before hunger sets in, their heart rate will slow and they well drift off to a sleep from which they never awaken. A mother who continues to

Renyard showing off his cast.

Kit thinks he is hiding.

nurse hopelessly impaired young does them a cruel disservice.

Kit still preferred the action of the daylight hours and continued to sleep with us at night. Then one morning, just as the darkness began to yield to dawn, I awoke with a start, certain someone had smacked my toe with a small hammer. Sadistically, Tom was chuckling. Before I could make my eyes focus, my ankle was hit again by that same small hammer. "Wah?" I managed to croak.

"Look Rae," said my wide-awake husband, "Look at Kit pounce!"

As I struggled to get my eyes to focus and my head into a viewing position, I could just make out Kit in the faint light of dawn. Tom wiggled his toe beneath the blanket and Kit's reactive pounce was nearly indescribable.

This little fellow would do well to weigh a pound, but he was lean and lanky of build. With more supple grace than any cat I had ever seen, Kit rose onto his hind legs, stretched to his full body length and then propelled himself into the air, powered by those deceptively strong legs. As the hind legs became airborne, he arched his body like a bow and brought his front paws tightly together—the hammer that had so rudely awakened me. A second before his front paws hit their target, his upper body because almost perfectly aligned with his front paws. The force of the blow was incredible for such a small animal. Immediately after the blow was struck, he lowered his nose to the blanket and scratched quickly, pulling his claws toward his body.

Foxes usually do not stalk their prey. They trot blithely over the meadow until they hear their quarry, which in most cases is the meadow mouse. Because of its speed and lightness of foot, the fox is generally right on top of the mouse when the confrontation begins. When the fox is that close, he simply pounces on the mouse with his forefeet, often breaking the mouse's back. If that fails and he already has the rodent pinned to the ground, he simply kills it with a quick bite. He then usually must scratch it out from under the grass with that quick, scratching motion of his forefeet. Other animalson the fox menu are woodchucks, squirrels, chipmunks and birds. Foxes also consume great quantities of crickets, fruits and corn. Foxes never seem to pass up the chance to kill weasels, moles, shrews and snakes, though they do not eat them unless they are on the brink of starvation.

Renyard's broken leg isn't much fun.

Almost every morning, at the crack of dawn, I was awakened by the increasingly familiar antics of Tom and Kit. Tom was overjoyed to have someone who functioned, as he did, at 4 a.m.

I saw a chance one morning to test Kit's hearing again. I jacked my knees up, making a tent of the blankets over them. Using my fingers I scratched lightly on the sheets beneath the canopy. No response from Kit. Again I scratched, only louder. Still no response. But if Kit saw the slightest movement of the blanket out of the corner of his eye, he'd pounce, dead-center on the hidden target every time.

We all tumbled downstairs; all but I wide awake. Tom, the dog and Kit went outside for their morning constitutionals while I groggily fixed coffee. When the others returned, they were followed by our Siamese cat, Pearl, "Me-ow"-ing proudly with a mouse dangling between her jaws. Making the typical mother cat's "dinner-is-served-for-my-baby" noises, Pearl marched across the floor and daintily dropped the furry morsel in front of Kit. I was frozen to my chair with awe. Our cat had long tolerated the various orphans but never had shown a desire to even casually fraternize. Kit sniffed the motionless mouse, then ate it with relish. I left the room, I can never handle such things before I'm fully awake, which usually is around 10 a.m.

A treat for Renyard.

Kit admires his bushy tail.

Pearl saw to it that Kit had a fresh mouse at least every other day, sometimes two a day. Kit's system had no problem digesting the mice and he was probably the better for it. Thanks to Pearl, Kit was learning that food came in different packages.

My daytimes were then devoted to building new pasture lines, repairing old fences and doing other outside chores. This day I had too much help: Dog and Kit, Week-o the goose, several raccoons, one skunk and nosy horses. I'd go to get a nail and electric fence insulator and find that the raccoons were playing with them. I'd go to pull a wire taut and Week-o would tug the wire with her beak in the opposite direction. I'd go to swing my hammer and a horse's nose would be thrust in front of me. All the while, Sweet-Pea, the skunk, would be between my feet, while Kit and the dog dashed frantically about the pasture. The job still got done.

It was at this time we laid claim to a motley flock of chickens: five bantams, four of which were roosters and six regular-sized chickens of mixed parentage, led by one huge Rhode-Island red rooster named Bill.

From the time Kit, then no bigger than a kitten, first ventured outdoors, the chickens would squawk continually. They knew instinctively, long before Kit himself realized it, that Kit was a fox.

Lately Kit was showing some interest in the chickens, perhaps because of their furious, attention-getting squawking and feather rustling. One day, we were relaxing outdoors when we noticed Kit following a bantam slowly and methodically across the lawn. By the time Kit was close enough to pose a threat to the bird, it suddenly took wing and flew to the safety of the barn. Kit just sat back on his haunches and watched, puzzled by the wonder of an airborne bird. When he noticed us watching, he feigned indifference as if to say, "I wasn't after that old chicken anyhow!"

Kit was already fleet-footed. He delighted in trying to teach the dog mid-air turns at full speed and his now-familiar pounce. A fox's natural gait is a trot of about six miles an hour. If pushed, it can maintain the trot at 26 miles an hour for short distances and foxes have been clocked loping at 45 miles an hour.

A few days later we watched Kit put his innate intelligence to productive use. He simply took off in a burst of speed and caught the bantam just as it was about to take wing. But the beating of the bird's wings about Kit's face so unnerved him that he released his prize. Kit sat down and thoughtfully scratched his left ear with his left hind foot. There was obviously a lot more to this hunting business than there seemed at first glance.

When Kit made his next attempt a few days later, he fared no better. The third time, so it's said, is charmed and so it was for Kit. He tenaciously held onto the chicken's neck, until it wore itself out from flapping. Too little to carry the bird away, Kit instead dragged it behind the barn, but he still had a big problem to cope with: his mouth and teeth weren't large enough to deliver a killing bite through all those feathers. He eventually worked his larger canine teeth through the veritable armor of feathers and severed the chicken's jugular vein. To some this may seem inhumane, but human laws do not pertain here. I have taken a bird away from a predator, only to see it immediately hunker down on the ground with neck outstretched, seemingly anxious to get it over with. To me, Kit's ability to learn to survive in the wild is just as important as that chicken's life. The chicken could also have lost its life to a fisher, hawk or to a human's hunger.

The big Rhode Island rooster, Bill, didn't tolerate any offense from any animal, let alone a pint-sized fox. Whenever Kit tried to test his stalking skills on Bill, the no-nonsense bird simply gave the obnoxious fox a lightning-fast peck with his beak, usually landing the blow sharply and painfully between his ears or on his nose. Bill never became a meal for Kit.

As time wore on, I noticed a subtle change in Kit's demeanor. With the hectic pace of the farm, one frequently notices things but we don't always pause to understand them. Kit was growing physically and mentally, slowly attaining foxhood. Those were not the things that had aroused my concern. Kit had taken to staying out until 10 or 11 o'clock at night. He would scratch at the door until he awakened one of us and

Kit looking for a friend.

then enter the house with an air of nonchalance. This smugness make us weary humans want to plant a swift kick on his derriere, but we simultaneously wanted to hug the rascal because he was safe.

But even that was not the real cause of my concern rather it was a subtle change in Kit, an undercurrent... a "sixth sense," if you will. After much thought and calculation, I thought I'd solved it.

Early the next morning, as Kit was playing "pounce" with Tom, I slowly and quietly made a small tent of the blankets by bending my legs at the knees. While Kit was wrestling with Tom, I scratched my fingers on the sheet beneath my bent knees. Kit immediately froze; ears swiveled toward me, wide and alert. Holding my breath in anticipation, I scratched lightly once again. Kit immediately launched himself into his classic pounce and came hammering down beneath my knees, his forepaws landing squarely on my fingers.

KIT COULD HEAR!

Kit romps at 4 months old.

Where's that mouse?

That is what my senses had detected and were trying to translate to my conscious during the preceding weeks. Kit's head was following the dictates of his ears, as they should in any normal animal. Until then, Kit's ears had always followed his eyes. Everything was at last functioning correctly in our little fox and his demeanor was proof of it.

Since our assorted group of chickens were given the run of the farm, they were at a higher risk of attack than a chicken who is safely penned up. When Kit added chicken to his food supply, he consumed about one bird every four weeks, but mice remained his natural and daily staple.

When I ventured into the woods or fields with Kit, I was invariably deluged with captured mice, moles and shrews. Mice are food to be tossed about very little, then quickly eaten. Moles and shrews are another matter. They are obviously beneath contempt, inedible but worthy of being tossed about and left lying at my feet, while Kit resumed the hunt.

I realize now that the rodent population must be enormous to support all the birds and mammals that prey on them for food. I didn't truly fathom that fact until I went walking with Kit. Now I can easily believe that the ground beneath my feet practically heaves and trembles with their numbers. On a fine July morning Kit could usually capture a mouse or other small rodent every five minutes in our hay field.

Would you like the mouse?

Kit's next step toward independence was to adopt a vacant space under the barn for his new, more private home. Kit had made a wise decision as his late evenings and early risings were about to earn banishment from our residence.

Over the preceding years, various animals had made a passageway that opened onto the main barn floor from under the structure. It wasn't uncommon to see the "under-the-barn" residents emerging, one after the other, from this opening. This year, Kit always came first, followed by four raccoons and one small skunk. There, they would join the "barn floor residents"—fawn, Canada goose, chickens and horses—in clamoring for food.

Kit was still in and out of the house during the day. Early in the mornings he came to get dog to come out and play. He quite frequently appeared at suppertime, hoping for leftovers.

One suppertime, the door not being securely latched, it opened easily at Kit's scratching. He came bounding in to find us eating his favorite human meal, chicken. Kit immediately trotted over to Chuck and began to whine. "No," said Chuck in his sternest voice. Kit then approached Tom and placed his paws on Tom's knee, which meant Kit's head was almost level with the table-top for an excellent whiff of chicken. "Down, Kit," grumbled Tom. Kit, now salivating, came to me, whined and yapped softly. "Kit, wait!" I said. Kit paced uneasily around the table, sniffing and whining. With a muted growl Kit nipped Tom on the ankle, fox talk for "Hurry up, Dad." Tom's displeasure was stated with a healthy slap on Kit's rump. Kit's eyes blazed, but he backed off. Kit then approached me again, whining and growling. When this pleading brought no results, he nipped me on the ankle. I immediately arose from my chair, bared my teeth, stared directly into his eyes and snarled and growled my displeasure. Kit looked at me wide-eyed for a moment, then dropped down onto his belly, his eyes never leaving my face. I pointed to the door and lowered my growl a half note. Kit slunk rapidly to the door. We finished our supper while Kit sat patiently and quietly for his turn at what was left of the chicken.

A wild animal, no matter how tamed by humans, follows his instinct. It is accepted etiquette to steal food from your siblings and your peers, if you can get away with it. Under the circumstances, Kit had kept himself under remarkable control.

While eating my supper I had received a phone call from the Rockport Police Department informing me that they had an injured fox. The fox was approximately three months old and had a broken front leg. I brought him home, treated him for shock and made an appointment with my veterinarians for the next morning.

When I brought the fox home from the vets' office, he was wearing a full leg cast. Kit and dog were playing in the barn and on our arrival they both came over to see what I had in my arms.

Kit was intrigued with this animal, but sadly for Kit, he would not be allowed to play and wrestle with one of his own kind. The new fox

Kit hopes Rosebud will play.

would have to be kept away from the rough and tumble lifestyle of the other inhabitants of this farm until his leg was healed.

A short time after the arrival of the injured fox, Kit made a home for himself under the barn, and articles of mine began to disappear: a pair of welding gloves that I was sure I had left on a cage, my gardening gloves and a favorite flannel shirt. At first I thought I was mistaken as to where I had left them, but when Kit snatched a wet shirt of mine from the laundry basket and streaked off for the barn before my own eyes, my suspicions were confirmed.

In the wild, Kit would have had his litter-mates with him. Their home would be full of each others' scents. I didn't begrudge Kit these items, for I was fairly sure he was using them to provide some smells of security. Later in the fall, as much as I dreaded the prospect, I could wiggle under the barn and retrieve the items. As it turned out, I would wiggle about beneath the barn sooner than I thought.

Kit wants the puppy to play.

Tom and I had spent part of a day rebuilding some of the doors to the horse stalls when we decided to drive into town on some errands and we would hang the doors when we returned. When we returned, Tom headed directly to the barn to hang the doors. Rather than take my things into the house, I slung my jacket and pocketbook onto the porch railing and went to help him.

A few minutes later, I was yelling in dismay at the sight of Dog and Kit scattering the contents of my pocketbook about the lawn. Kit grabbed my green leather wallet and went racing away through the woods with dog in hot pursuit.

Ordinarily, I never keep more than ten dollars or so in my wallet, but I had been hoarding every spare dollar for car insurance and was within twenty dollars of the needed amount. The bill was due in four days.

In vain, I searched the dooryard, the wooded paths and back pasture.

I continued to search into the darkness with a flashlight. I tried to convince myself that the light might reflect my small, moss-green wallet in the clutter of grass, twigs and leaves. I pointed the flashlight through the holes in the rocks that formed the foundation of the barn, locating the raccoons' nest, the skunk's nest and finally Kit's home. I could tell it was Kit's nest, for there lay my flannel shirts, welding gloves and other articles. My wallet didn't appear to be there.

The next morning, I reluctantly donned my one-piece denim jumpsuit, removed a couple of rocks in the foundation wall and wriggled my way into that dirty, dank space.

When at last I had crawled my way into Kit's section, the flashlight revealed all the items I had seen the night before ... and my wallet! Eagerly, I snatched it up, bundled everything together except for one shirt and wormed my way back into the fresh air and daylight.

As I opened my wallet my heart sank. It was completely empty. No driver's license, pictures or, most critically, the money!

The odds were extremely good that the money was lying somewhere on the ground about the building. It would be found eventually, but I had a deadline only a few days away and I doubted the insurance company would take much stock in my excuse.

In desperation I began to haunt Dog and Kit's play areas and trails. Luck, in a most unexpected form, came my way with the insurance date only 24 hours away.

A wounded songbird fluttered onto our lawn and Kit caught it. I presumed he would immediately kill it, but instead he carried it proudly about perhaps trying to tease Dog. I did not enjoy hearing the bird's cries of fear, so I took off in pursuit of Kit. Kit, fearing that I wanted the bird for my own lunch, headed for the woods along one of his well-worn paths. I didn't expect to keep up with him, but hoped he would put the bird out of its misery sooner if he thought I wanted it. As I leaped over a log in the path, I stopped short, for lying on the ground in plain sight was my money! All of it, still folded as it had been when it was in my wallet.

As the days of September rolled away, Kit became more and more uneasy in the human environment. It became rare for him to be seen by anyone but me and the dog. His ability to suddenly appear and disappear in front of my eyes never ceased to amaze me. Kit had learned the fine art of blending into the landscape.

October is dispersal month. Young foxes leave their parents and establish their own territories. We did not know it then, but Dog and I enjoyed Kit's company for the last time on October the fourth, a cool, dry Friday.

Dog missed his friend and companion. Each morning for several months, he would sniff and look about their old, favorite haunts. Sometimes he would sniff so eagerly that we thought perhaps Kit had visited us during the night. Once the snow came, the dog ceased his active searching for Kit.

The next spring, as I was raking the lawn free of winter debris, I found one of Dog's missing flea collars. Calling him to me I showed him his old collar saying, "Dog, here's one of the flea collars that was lost when you and Kit were playing." Dog's ears came to immediate attention. "Kit?" I repeated, and Dog immediately and joyously went bounding across the lawn searching for Kit.

A few minutes later, a sad dog returned, lay down at my feet and sighed.

Doesn't anyone want to play today?

Time to go to the vet again.

Broken wing friend.

Chapter 7
Birds of a Feather

Rehabilitators who specialize in birds have my admiration and my blessing.

Baby birds who have not acquired feathers must be kept under a light placed 10-12 inches above them for warmth, and fed every half hour from dawn to dusk. It is a demanding, exhausting task.

Once they have acquired feathers and until they actually fly, they require feeding only every hour. Baby birds with developing feathers are called fledglings.

For baby songbirds, a good feeding recipe is an egg, baby cereal and milk stirred and cooked to a consistency that will stay on the end of a toothpick. Baby hawks and owls might require hamburg mixed with dog or cat hair and ground chicken bones mixed in to suit their specific dietary needs. Eventually, the young meat-eaters graduate to mice, squirrels and other small animals. Rehabilitators find some of these morsels on our highways, known as road kills. As a rehabilitator stops his vehicle to retrieve a road kill, he or she usually receives some very odd glances from the other passing motorists. If one has a healthy budget, such stares can be prevented by ordering dead, frozen mice from a medical research laboratory and having them delivered to your doorstep by United Parcel Service.

If you should find a baby bird or birds, upon the ground, try desperately to locate its nest and replace the bird. If you locate the tree but can't get the bird back into its nest, build a make-shift nest. To do this take a square-foot piece of hardware cloth, one-inch mesh chicken wire, metal mosquito screening or a wire basket and cup it into a nest shape. Fasten it securely into or onto the tree. Fill the cup with dry, not green, leaves and grass, wedging them through the wire. Leave the center of the nest lower than the rim so that it is cup shaped. If you have the original nest put it in the center. The baby bird's chances of survival are better here than in an even more foreign environment, including the ground.

In the wild, two out of three birds die in their first year. Predation and disease are the principal causes. Baby birds raised by humans have the same fatality rate.

I find that raising birds and mammals simultaneously presents a definite conflict. I spend my spare time taking the mammals into the fields and woods, trying to accustom them to their natural environment. Having a baby bird or two in the house seems to allow me only sufficient time to get to the barn and back before it's bird feeding time again.

A flegling robin that came to live with us one year was promptly named "Rockin' Robin". He was as cheerful asthe robin's song and was nobody's fool, adopting each of us in the family as "mother". Upon seeing any human within a six-foot radius, he would let out a loud "Cheer-up" and open his little beak to awesome dimensions, just as he would to demand food of his real mother.

In the cage next to his were two fledgling cedar wax-wings. Unlike Rockin' Robin, they constantly uttered their off-key baby calls, whether they were hungry or not. Their nerve-wracking ability to create a constant din amazed me, so I devoted some time to a careful study of them, hoping to find a clue to their persistent raucousness.

We named them "Tweedle-dum" and Tweedle-dee". First, Tweedle-dum would give his high-pitched screech, followed immediately by Tweedle-dee giving his screech, then they would break into a screeching duet. This was repeated again and again with neither little fellow seeming to tire or lose volume. I became so inured to the constant din that when I turned out the lights at night, the immediate cessation of noise startled me to the extent that I wondered for a moment what household machinery had stopped running.

As fledglings grow their flight feathers, they exercise their muscles by flapping their wings, eventually raising themselves off their perch. At this time they need room to fly. Although the ability to fly is instinctive and need not be taught, birds so not have the innate, delicate skill required to land from full flight on a narrow tree limb.

The cedar wax-wings swooped about the room, navigating the enclosed area with relative ease. But when they swooped down to land upon a wooden chair-back, for instance, they would invariably miss the slat by an inch. After several tries, they had that minor problem resolved. Let them try to land on a house plant, however, and when they made contact with the stem, the bending action from their weight toppled

The loud babies.

them off into scrabbling free-flight.

Rockin' Robin preferred Tom's hat or his broad shoulders from which to survey his kingdom. As he became more expert at flight, he loved to have Tom walking about. A moving target put more spice into the exercise. As he landed safely upon Tom's head or shoulders he would sing his "Cheer-up!"

Release time arrives when a bird is able to fly and land adequately. It must also know enough to look down, not up, for his meal.

When it was time for the cedar wax-wings to be released, my friend Christine and I decided to free them in an apple orchard four miles from our house. We reasoned that the orchard, brim-full of their own, gregarious kind, would be more suitable than our farm, where the birds are seldom seen.

Tweedle-dum and Tweedle-dee flitted off together going from tree to tree. With joy in our hearts and a sense of accomplishment we returned to my house for a cup of coffee, uninterrupted by wax-wing noises.

At six o'clock the next morning, as I was returning from putting the horses out to pasture, I found myself frozen in mid-step by a familiar call. My eyes slowly followed my disbelieving ears, and there, perched high on the telephone wire, were Tweedle-dum and Tweedle-dee!

Every morning for a week they were there to greet me with their raucous calls before finally flying off through the morning mist one day, never to return.

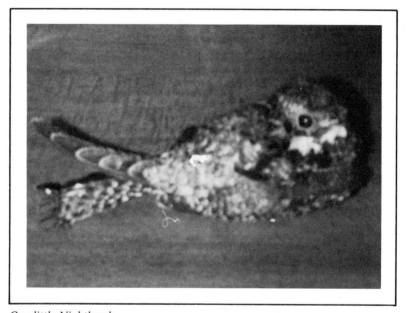

Our little Nighthawk.

Chapter 8
ET and Friends

My typical day starts early, sometimes much too early if I have been giving night feedings.

When I arise, I prepare many different breakfasts, for the squirrels (red, grey and flying), baby birds and the injured animals who may be house-bound because of the close supervision they require. We require breakfast, too.

From April through August of one year alone, 32 orphans have come to stay with us: squirrels, woodchucks, foxes, fawns, raccoons, skunks, porcupines, ducks, robins, night-hawks, cedar wax-wings.

I prepare dishes of dry and canned dog food for the raccoons, skunks and foxes who are anxiously waiting outside. They share unless they are very young. Some are fed separately, as was Prickles the porcupine... for obvious reasons. He was kept caged unless a human was around to chaperone.

I then go do the horse chores, bringing with me warm milk for the fawns and table scraps for the sea gull.

Orphan wildlife are raised on a variety of formulas. Highlights of the weekly grocery list might include raw cows' milk, powdered infant formula, eggs, lots of canned dog food, even more dry dog food and several loaves of whole wheat bread.

Depending on the age and species of the orphans, feeding times may be from every hour to every four hours. Some must be fed throughout the day and night for a few weeks.

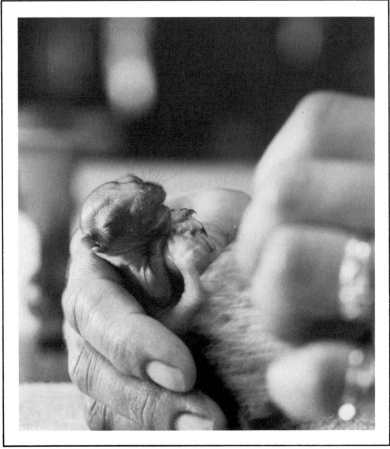

E.T. is pink and sticky at one week old.

By the time I've finished those chores, I run back to the house for a welcome cup of coffee while doing some of the household chores. Three to four hours go by in the wink of an eye and then it's feeding time again.

My human friends are very special. They are well tested by the things they must put up with around our house. A quiet evening of playing cards, for instance, may well involve an interruption or two to bottle feed some of the orphans. Occasionally, the card game is disrupted permanently.

Late one evening, Warden Allen appeared with a fawn who had been struck by a motorcycle. The kitchen table was immediately cleared of coffee cups and cards so we could examine the fawn under decent lighting conditions. His injuries consisted of cuts and one major bruise. We all adjourned to the barn to place him in a horse stall, which necessitated moving an injured fox to a smaller pen. When the fawn was settled down, we all retired to the house for coffee and conversation.

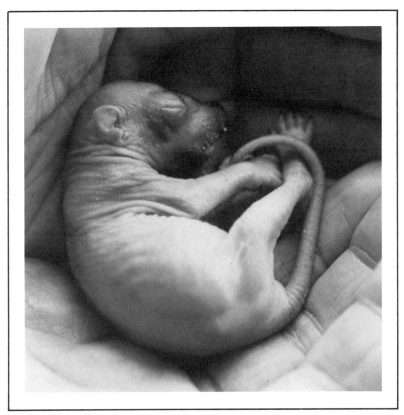

Little orphan E.T.

By midnight everyone was home and abed, except for me and probably the wardens. I was feeding one lucky little fawn a warm bottle of milk.

Although my fort-82- is raising the orphans, I am learning to take care of the injured. Another fox, Renyard was three months old when he was struck by a car while out hunting with his parents. His left front leg sustained a compound fracture. By the time I got to the town to pick him up, the fox was so traumatized that he was on the verge of shock. I squirted several syringes of glucose onto the back of his tongue. Plastic hypodermic syringes used without a needle are excellent feeders for wildlings. Within a few moments, I had him beside me in the car so that I could talk to him constantly and massage him gently whenever possible as I drove. Because of his unstable condition, I brought him straight home and made an appointment with our veterinarians for the next morning. A leg as damaged as his should be set as soon as possible, but if I had taken him that first day he probably would not have survived the trip because of the extreme stress he was under. Even though he was in severe pain, near-normal body functions returned within a few hours.

The next morning, after he'd had a light breakfast of canned dog food, I gave him a helping of sugar-water to help combat the stress he would endure from his ride to the veterinarians' office. I was nearly to the office when Renyard started panting frantically. As soon as I drove into the parking lot and stopped, I have him some more cold sugar-water which he eagerly lapped down.

Renyard's eyes were glazed with pain but not a sound or a move did he make as the cast was applied to his leg and a light dose of pain medication was administered. As Dr. Tricia stroked his beautiful fur and talked to him, his eyes cleared of the pain, and the beautiful tawny-gold eyes shined back at her with a look of gratitude. Our ride home was somewhat more relaxed than the one to the office.

For a wild, young animal, he was extremely gentle. Renyard would show his fear of humans by snarling upon their approach, but when he found that didn't deter me, he would settle for whining as I handled him.

His name was given to him by a young child's "nonsense jingle" rhyming barnyard, henyard and foxy Renyard.

I was more than amazed at his ability to accept his second trip to the vets for another cast change. To submit to my ministrations here, at home, was difficult for him, and now he must trust a stranger. Although we could see and smell his fear, he accepted the vet's handling. When Dr. Rose at last had the new cast on, she received the highest accolade from Renyard! A quick lick or two on the fingers. Four weeks later Tom and I removed the final cast. Renyard spent an enjoyable thirty minutes gleefully scratching, digging and biting that itchy leg. A cloud of dead hair drifted about his smiling face.

Although, at first, Renyard walked and ran with a very pronounced limp, it gradually improved until there was only the slightest hint of a limp at the walk.

Within a week of Renyard's cast being removed, I released him from his pen. He now had complete freedom to leave or to stay; the decision was completely up to him. Renyard chose to stay.

Several mornings later Tom came in with a look of amazement on his face and wonderment in his eyes. He had witnessed something secretive and magical. He had been out in the barn before dawn, and sensed that something was happening in the paddock behind the barn. Tom tip-toed to the back corner of the barn and strained to see into the darkness. He occasionally heard the soft padding of feet, and the almost soundless woof that a happy fox makes. (The sound is close to that of a human breath blowing out a match.) As the sky slowly lightened, he could see their outlines, Renyard and Kit, shadow boxing. At times they moved so swiftly and dropped to the ground so quickly that he would lose sight of them. Then they would reappear like specters from out of the the ground, to rise and pirouette about each other. The only sounds to be heard were their occasional soft woofs and their footpads falling upon the sand.

E.T. looking for his kitty.

E.T. sneaking up on Duchess.

E.T. helping Barbara with lunch.

They played there often in the very early dawn, and sometimes just before total darkness fell in the evening. I, too, got to watch this incredible display of grace and beauty.

The animals who have had the ability to deter Tom from his work have been few. The foxes, Kit and Renyard, could dissuade Tom quite easily from his chores, as could one of the smallest of our visitors, a tiny mammal named "Zippy".

She was brought to us by our cat, Pearl. As Pearl laid her prize on the floor it began to crawl away. I won the ensuing race to Pearl's intended supper by the length of a cat's claw. My son, Bruce, removed the irate cat to the other side of the door as I opened my hands to see what she'd brought. It was tiny enough to fit easily into the palm of my hand. It was seal grey in color, with the softest, finest fur. Its eyes were dark, liquid brown. The soft, upright ears were curved attentively toward the sound of my voice. The tail was broad and flat with a rounded tip. What I held in my hand was a flying squirrel. She was evidently still young enough to automatically go limp if picked up by the scruff of the neck by her mother, or in this case, our cat. She wasn't injured in any way, probably because our cat seized her. Pearl assumed her meal to be already dead because of the lack of resistance and didn't deliver a killing bite.

Since I was in the middle of fixing supper, I needed a temporary home for our new guest. I slid her gently down into Tom's shirt pocket. The pocket would be dark and warm and the beating of Tom's heart should give her added security.

As we were finishing our supper, Tom's pocket began to tremble gently. Soon, a pair of dark-brown eyes were scanning us and the surroundings from just above the edge of Tom's pocket.

While I was turning a 20-gallon aquarium into a suitable home for the squirrel by adding a small hollow log, dried grasses, a few seeds and nuts, a hard-boiled egg and water, Zippy sat scanning her new environment, but now from the vantage point of Tom's shoulder.

The little squirrel made herself at home, in the aquarium and out. Her favorite hangout was in Tom's pocket, but in the evenings she put Tom to work. She would get Tom to hold his arm straight up in the air with his hand cocked parallel to the floor, a perfect diving platform. She would center herself on his palm, bend her front legs while weaving her body to the left, straighten up, again bend her front legs and weave her body to the right, staighten up once more and finally launch herself into space, gliding to a landing on the couch. With incredible speed she would zip across the couch, leap onto Tom's pant leg, race up his body and arm and come to a standstill on his palm, ready to repeat the entire procedure. This game lasted as long as Tom's arm could be held up.

Flying squirrels do not fly; they glide. The flying squirrel has loose folds of skin on both sides of its body which extend from the outside of the wrists on the front legs to the ankles on the hind legs. When the squirrel launches himself into the air, he stretches his legs out to the side and the folds of skin become taut. The squirrel becomes a mini-parachute, using his tail as the steering rudder. Since the squirrel can only glide, the farther away his landing target is, the higher up he must take off. If the landing target is quite close, the squirrel will lose very little altitude. If the target—usually a tree—is farther away, the squirrel may land quite close to its base. If the flying squirrel should land on the ground, he will find it very slow going through the underbrush, for the shape of his body and the shortness of his legs impede his progress through the grass and other tangles.

As for Zippy's odd calisthenics on Tom's palm before take-off, I finally found the answer to their function in an old animal behavior book. Zippy was triangulating, a method of surveying an area.

Unlike the more adventuresome red and grey squirrels, Zippy wouldn't leave Tom's body unless she and he were in very familiar surroundings. Tom could do most of his chores with Zippy along if he chose. We could visit friends for dinner with Zippy along. Taking care of Zippy was very easy this way, but how were we to release him if he was so literally attached to us? Tom was not about to take up residence in a hollow tree! After intense searching, it appeared that an old elm tree in our dooryard held some flying squirrels. The best plan seemed to involve Tom,

Zippy's most trustworthy human friend. He put in some pre-dawn time sitting at the base of that tree, helping Zippy feel secure enough to start exploring the tree. By the end of the week, she ventured high enough to discover some holes in that tree and some new friends. She never came back down.

We had been so positive that Zippy was going to be very difficult to return to the wild, but we learned preconceptions and appearances are not always solid in these cases. Yet, I still occasionally prejudge an animal.

E.T., the grey squirrel, couldn't have been more than 24 yours old when he was delivered to me. His pink body was about three inches long and sticky to the touch. I kept him nestled on top of a blanket under which was a heating pad, feeding him four or five drops of formula every hour. I was so certain that he was a hopeless cause that I did not feed him through the night.

Against all odds, he was still alive and thriving one week later. He didn't look like much. He was bright pink, but the stickiness had dissipated. Grey squirrels' eyes open in about their fifth week and they are fully furred by that time. E.T.'s eyes were open at five weeks; he was growing beautifully; he even had a squirrel vocabulary that didn't quit! He was a spoiled brat and very normal except for one thing. He still didn't have any hair. You cannot begin to conceive just how homely a squirrel is without hair! The game wardens would pick him up and examine the number of toes, his teeth and eyes; all agreed he had to be a grey squirrel, hair or no. I was getting very helpful comments— "Do you know anyone who makes Barbie doll clothes?"—but in truth this hairlessness was not funny, as E.T.'s odds of contracting pneumonia were compounded by this lack of natural protection.

E.T. continued to grow and thrive, except for his lack of hair. When he was three months old, he was still as smooth as a billiard ball, with some fine fuzz growing here and there. E.T. loved to be outdoors, playing and riding about in my pocket, but within a short while he would become chilled and need his warm blanket and heating pad.

In August, I was called for jury duty. Most all of the orphans were capable of going six hours between meals, except for the cedar waxwings and E.T. Thank goodness for my friend and neighbor, Christine. She volunteered to take over the care of these babies. Christine isn't a lady of leisure. She helps milk 80 head of Holsteins twice a day and does enough other chores daily to equal the average person's weekly work schedule.

E.T. stayed with Christine for almost two months. After my jury duty was fulfilled, I had six weeks of work picking apples. E.T. was perfectly happy. He had two mothers and one of Christine's kittens of his own to play with. Babies are babies and when they are young they don't realize whether they are carnivores or vegetarians. My fully-grown cats pretty much ignore the orphans we raise, youngsters that otherwise would be fair game for them. Whether this is because they realize that I would

Timothy, the grey squirrel.

break their necks for going after one of the orphans or the fact that the orphans have a distinct human smell overlayed with their natural smell that restrains my cats, I don't know.

E.T. playing with the kitten was a sight to behold! He would scurry about the rooms looking for his kitten and when he found her he would race up and over her body with glee, leaving the kitten with a startled, helpless look. The kitten would immediately chase after him, but E.T. was faster than she and his knack for launching himself off furniture only confused the kitten. Within a short while, the kitten would be huffing and puffing in exhaustion, while E.T. would be none the worse for the frenzy. Soon they would be sitting together, resting and waiting to see which one would start the next round.

E.T. became a full-fledged squirrel while in Christine's care. He began to consume some solid food with his formula and one day simply refused any more formula. E.T.'s body grew more thin fuzz and his tail became a respectable, fluffy grey squirrel tail, which only made him look more bizarre.

The handicap of not having a fur coat caught up with E.T. Christine called one evening to tell me he was refusing food. He also was lying on her shoulder, crying constantly to her. I suspected pneumonia and our suspicions were confirmed a few hours later. E.T. was a very sick squirrel for a few days, but he recovered. This little guy was determined to live, despite the odds.

By the first of November, E.T. came home to stay. He had a brand-new home designed just for him, a cage five and a half feet tall, sixteen inches deep and two feet wide. It was equipped with a climbing tree. The cage was a compromise between what E.T. needed and what would fit into the spare space of our dining room. E.T. liked his new cage, but he just wasn't his loud, sometimes obnoxious, self. Bruce had referred to E.T.'s stay at Christine's as "summer camp" because he had learned so many new things there and had such a good time. When I mentioned how subdued E.T. was acting, Bruce informed me that it was all my fault; I had sent him to summer camp! Perhaps he was right.

By the end of the month, E.T. was again his loud, talkative, demanding self. Now, at long last, he had a coat of squirrel grey fur all over his body. It was thin, but it was there and improving with age.

One morning, as I came in from doing chores, I found E.T. screaming in pain. The only thing I could see was that he wasn't using one of his hind legs properly. E.T. made his first trip to the vet's office.

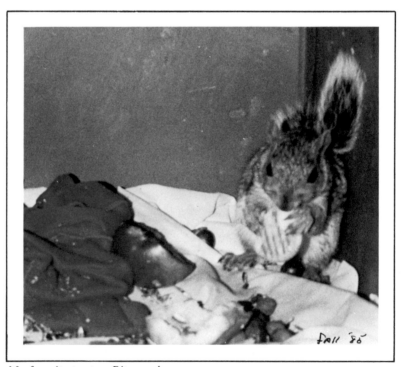

My favorite treat, a Ritz cracker.

Enjoying a sunflower seed.

Everyone was on hand to meet the little squirrel that they had heard so much about. E.T. proceeded to charm everyone, between the nerve-wracking waves of pain. It was discovered that he had broken one of his hind legs. A broken leg needs a splint, but what do you use for a splint on a leg that small? Nothing confounds a country vet for long. Dr. Tricia thought of the answer after a few moments: Cow teat dilaters. I held E.T. in the palm of my hand, tummy-side up, while Dr. Tricia straightened his leg and applied the cast. Our hands are small but they seemed incredibly big for this tiny job! Eventually, the cast was completed and what a cast it was: E.T. even had a walking heel.

E.T. accepted the cast about as well as any human child. He hated it with a passion. When he wasn't raving and ranting about it, he cried piteously. When he reached the crying stage, one of us would retrieve him from his cage and try to amuse him. He liked to crawl into my shirt pocket and peek out at the passing scenery as I went about my house-work. He was treated to special foods like grapes and cauliflower. Thankfully he didn't chew the cast off, which well he could have. Six weeks literally crawled by and the cast was finally removed. It was a toss-up as to who was the most thankful.

As the days moved toward spring, so did E.T.'s coat move toward a semblance of a real squirrel coat. It was as good andthick as any squirrel's coat. Definite plans were made to change E.T.'s lifestyle in the month of June.

During the warm days of April and May, E.T. was outdoors in a cage or on our shoulders getting accustomed to the smells and sounds of the outdoors. It was pretty intimidating to him at first, but soon his gung-ho nature asserted itself.

I have three shrubs six to eight feet high that are grouped together and serve me well as starter trees for many of the clambering wildlife. They can climb and explore but are not out of my reach entirely, plus the shrubs give them some safety so that after one or two explorations I can leave them for a bit. I felt that E.T. was more than ready for the challenge of the shrubs.

"More than ready" turned out to be an understatement. E.T. leaped into that shrub as though he knew what he was doing. Perhaps he did. He raced up one side and down the other; he leaped from limb to limb and branch to branch. E.T., as usual, felt he had the world by the tail on a downhill cant, but oops! Through the leaves he fell, clawing and digging trying to stop his fall. He was fast running out of tree when he managed to get a grip on a small branch. After scrambling back onto a branch sufficiently large to hold his weight, he looked rather crestfallen. Then he started to chirp and sputter as only a squirrel can. I was clearly at fault, for I had neglected to inform him that a cluster of leaves only looks solid. He felt it wasn't very sporting of me to let him find out the hard way!

I then suggested that he had enough for today and held out my arm for him to climb onto. NO SIR-E-E!! He was going to stay and master that tree, and I was welcome to leave; he was doing just fine, thank you!

I was finding the whole exercise rather boring, so I left him and went into the house to make a fast sandwich, keeping an eye on this cocky squirrel.

E.T. was still running about the shrub, but with a little more caution. He wasn't missing me a bit. Perhaps, I mused, this release is going to be easier than I expected. About that time, a robin decided to land on one of the branches of the shrub that E.T. was so noisily careening about. E.T. instantly froze. The robin was quietly preening its feathers when suddenly it burst into song! The presence of the bird had evidently intimidated E.T., but the bird's choral display paniced the squirrel. He began to scream. The robin left hurriedly as I approached, but all E.T. wanted was the immediate safety of my shirt. He was a blur of speed as he leaped onto my arm, raced up my sleeve and plummeted into the safety of my pocket. Life in the great outdoors was not as simple as it may have seemed.

The next day's outing was easier and the outings thereafter a snap. The following next week, I graduated E.T. to the real thing, the big oak tree. He loved it. He spent the whole day there and when evening came

Getting ready to land.

Touchdown.

he initially didn't want to come down. The next day, I rigged a box up in the tree with his blanket, water bottle and some food. At dusk he refused to come to me but chose instead to remain in his box. He used his box as a home until sometime in July when that, too, was no longer needed. E.T. probably moved deeper into the surrounding woods where the food was more abundant and there would be more squirrels for him to associate with.

Chapter 9
Bud, Bucky and Others

It is late fall and this old farm is bedding itself down for the winter. The animals number only a few now, the domestic stock of horses, cats and the dog. The wildlings are two whitetail deer and a male raccoon.

The raccoon is called "Bud" and he has been here since he was six weeks of age. At three months, he and his brother "Weiser" were leading the normal lives of raccoons, as were the four older raccoons I was raising. Bud and Weiser were spending their nights exploring the pastures and brooks of Willow-Brook. Exactly what happened we'll never know. They were still at the age where they should be returning every day to the farm, but they were missing for four consecutive days, and then only Bud returned. His actions translated roughly into "scared out of his wits". He spent the first week of his return refusing to leave the barn unless he was with me or the dog. After the first week, he would come to the house on his own during the daytime, but he still refused to go roaming with the four older raccoons at night.

Bud is six months old now, weighs 19 pounds, is 20 inches long excluding tail and is 12 inches high. The four other raccoons have dispersed into the wild, but Bud's territory consists only of the barn, the path to the house and the house itself. I am hoping that his mating urge will push him back into the wild. The mating season is during February and March.

Because of his hefty size, we must keep Bud away from small children, as well as adults who have not been introduced to the techniques of playing with a half-grown raccoon and still keeping your face, fingers and toes intact. Bud is trying to play as gently as he knows how, yet soft human skin unprotected by fur is extremely vulnerable.

If Bud doesn't come down the ladder from the hayloft as I am doing the morning chores, Dog will wait impatiently for him while I go back to the house. Dog's day is not right until the two of them have gotten together, preferably in the house to play. I used to take my mid-morning shower while they played until Bud and Dog created too much havoc, even for me. After rumpling up the freshly made bed "rumpling" is too kind a word—they would then turn their attention to the clothes basket. I would leave my morning bath to find half my morning household chores undone. The final straw was when Bud discovered that if he wormed his way up under the shower curtains and stole the container of hair shampoo, the liquid soap or some other such goodie, I would leap out of the tub and pursue him about the house. As I was rescuing the shampoo or cleaning up the mess, he would plunge into MY bathtub full of warm, steamy water! Not only did he create a huge, sloppy mess by whipping the wet facecloth about in his teeth, but he was thoroughly disrupting one of the few calm and enjoyable times of my day! From that day onward, no four-footer has been allowed in the house during my bath time!

Dog is not above pulling a few sneaky tricks, either. After what I consider a sufficient playtime, I cagily wait my chance to grab Bud when he isn't looking, so he can be put outside. Bud has a built-in time clock so he is already waiting for the maneuver. Sensing that the time is approaching to go out, he will crawl under the couch for a nap. Having finally outwaited him and outsmarted him, I attempt to place him outside the door as he cunningly wraps his forelegs tightly about my neck and makes distressing and pitiful sounds. I harden my heart, deafen my ears and un-cling him from my body. I gently place him down on the top of a tall box at the farther end of the porch, thus enabling me to beat him back to the door. Within 20 minutes or so, Dog will come to me and tell me that he desperately needs to go out, as evidenced by his agitated whining. I go and open the door to let Dog out; Dog then proceeds to come to a standstill halfway through the door just long enough to let his lonesome friend, Bud, back inside. Dog immediately joins Bud in another romp throughout the house! I hate to admit how many times I've fallen for that charade.

The two deer came this spring. The doe, Princess, was rescued by Warden Thompson. She had come out of the woods and was nuzzling a fisherman's pickup truck which she refused to abandon under any circumstances. Warden Thompson was called to the scene and upon examining the fawn realized that she was physically unfit to remain in the wild, at least for the present time. We found her to be approximately two months old, undernourished, totally blind in one eye and partially blind in the other. We will never know if she was born this way or if the disabilities were caused, as they often are, by a collision with a vehi-

Ok, where's the bottle, John?

cle. By the next morning, she had contracted pneumonia, due not only to her physical condition but also to the stress of being handled by humans. Unfortunately, it became a two-person job to restrain her long enough to give her the required twice-daily injections for the pneumonia. Deer, even when tame have an instinctive fear of being restrained in any manner.

The male, "Bucky", was two days old when he was brought to us by the wardens. He was picked up by well-meaning humans who thought he was an orphan because they didn't see his mother. Deer fawns and seal pups are purposefully left alone for up to five hours before their mothers return to feed them. The young fawns are born without any scent so as to protect them from predators while their mothers are fully scented and, if near their young, could attract predators.

Most of the wildlife who are picked up are in reality not orphans! Their mothers care for them as intensely as any human mother. With the loss of her baby, the mother doe will often bleat piteously for hours.

If you should see what you think is an orphan, LOOK and OBSERVE! If at all possible, go a little distance away and observe for at least a half-hour. If a baby is floundering around in an environment that it normally wouldn't be in, it's probably an orphan. Most babies have siblings and they, too, should be in the same area if everything is normal.

Because it's hard to generalize for different species with different habits, it is best to get a warden or humane society person to help you. If time is on your side, call them and explain the situation. Above all, don't collect a crowd!

If you rescue an orphan, do no more than keep it warm and if necessary, give it glucose. Get it to a rehabilitator or veterinarian. Immediately!! Don't assume that becauseit appears healthy you can keep it and enjoy it for a few days. The needs of these young are many. They need a specialized diet (still a tremendous shock to the system because it's foreign, not its own natural milk) and frequent feedings (the amounts and times depending on its age and specie.) Most orphans, what is more, cannot urinate or defecate on their own. It will need antibiotics for stress and the germs found in its new environment.

Ignorance is at work too often. Well-meaning folks who thought it was so easy to adopt a wildling end up bringing it to us several days later on the edge of death. Most of these animals are suffering from diarrhea and pneumonia.

We realize and we understand. Oh, how well we understand and sympathize, but all too often, we the rehabilitators get to watch the animal die!

Bucky is a fine looking youngster this fall. He has little spike horns to show off to the humans who come to admire him. Fawns, male and female, spend their entire first year with their mothers, frequently into the next fall. Bucky, being the normal, healthy deer that he is, hates being penned up. I try to get him out as much as possible into our woods

Sarah and a special friend.

and fields. It's a hard process, since a deer's time to roam is from late evening to early morning. Bucky will only accept me as his walking companion since I am his "mother". He never goes more than 100 yards from where I am standing. Bucky must have a chance to browse as he ambles along, so I spend a lot of time standing in one spot. Unless I am helping Tom brush out a new woods road, it can get terribly boring for me. During such time, I take a book along to read, several pages at a time before I move on to another locale. Bucky's first rainstorm wasn't appreciated by either of us. I couldn't very well read and I was getting cold and damp from the slow pace, while Bucky was shaking his head, stamping his feet and generally resenting the funny feeling the rain was creating on his head and body.

Until he was three months old, I couldn't afford the luxury of passing the time with a book. Instead, I perched myself on a rock or tree limb, swatted mosquitoes and kept my eyes on Bucky. At the snap of a twig, honk of a car horn, bark of a dog or the unannounced sweep of a breeze, Bucky would immediately drop down into the surrounding grasses and ferns, disappearing instantly from sight. At first he would stay hidden until I went to him. The ability of a cinnamon-colored coat, peppered with white spots, to blend so harmoniously into the greens of the spring grasses and ferns, yellows of the buttercups and the brown leaves of yesteryear is incredible.

Now that late fall is here, our farming neighbors have more time to drop by for a bit of socializing. First they want to see how the two fawns are growing. Later, as we stand about in the dooryard, I'll see their eyes flick across the lawn and scan the pasture and they will quietly ask after the foxes, Kit and Renyard.

Some of these farmers once looked on foxes strictly as pests, just another wild animal looking for a free meal from their chicken flock, not to mention a possible carrier of rabies. They routinely shot them.

Since meeting Kit and Renyard and watching them grow to adults, most of the farmers look upon the foxes differently. Now the fox has a personality and conjures up images of intelligence, beauty and grace. They've watched Kit and Renyard hunt the field mice and have come to realize that maybe foxes do more good than harm. Maybe they are even worth a chicken or two.

Late fall is when I find myself mulling over the past year's events in detail. I think first of the failures. I examine all the events leading to an animal's death to see if perhaps I could have done something differently to improve its chances for survival. If I feel that something could have been changed, I place that thought on my mental shelf of new ideas. After that mental chore is finished, I try to put those painful memories away, forever.

If you ever have a chance to talk and listen to a rehabilitator, you will hear stories that are informative, surprising, charming and hilarious. There will be little, if any, talk of the failures. Raising orphan wildlife means long hours, hard work, no pay and very little appreciation.

A dream come true.

A rehabilitator learns to maintain a positive frame of mind by concentrating on his successes as much as possible. A rehabilitator learns that each animal is an individual; it has a story to tell and a lesson to teach.

Every specie fills a clearly-defined need in our ecological system, therefore their biological and physical structures enable them to exist within certain limits. But each animal is an individual and has a personality of its own. We also fit this mold. We also have physical, mental and biological limits. Man, without mechanical aids, can never fly as the eagle or gambol in the seas as the porpoise.

The rest of my winter will be spent reliving the good times and the successes and looking forward to spring.

Come spring, I will become a grandmother for the first time. It seems like only yesterday my boys were babies. I think of the wondrous experiences this farm held for the boys, and soon for our grandchild.

Years ago, I set myself a goal that each year I would learn a new skill. One year it was sewing, another year it was kayaking and another learning and working as a rough carpenter. As my boys grew, I learned to hunt and fish. The thrill of skateboarding was mine until our oldest son, Chuck, broke his arm and he and Bruce took the skateboard away. I've broken and trained my own horse for trail riding and then showing at halter and now she, too, will present me with a new and untried challenge this spring, her first foal and my first foaling.

Spring will bring us a grandchild, a new foal and wildlife orphans.

And now, as I walk to the barn on this crisp November morning, I see the weeping willow shorn of all its leaves and bare of saucy raccoon faces. The lawn is still green, but the beautiful, fiery red glow of the foxes' coats no longer glide over it.

As I go about my chores, memories of the orphans eddy and flow about me. I am saddened by their departures, yet gladdened by their independence. So with tears in my eyes and a smile on my face, I watch the sunrise, feeling very much at peace in my world.

Helen and Rosebud getting acquainted.

DATE DUE			
2			
5 8			
JUN 8			
7/19			
7/26			
8/9			
5/23			
9/26			
1-19			
6/1			
10/19			

Perry, Rae
    14353

Wild Friends